i

WOMEN AND THE FEMININE PRINCIPLE
IN THE WORKS
OF
PAUL CLAUDEL

Women and the Feminine Principle in the Works of Paul Claudel

ANN BUGLIANI

studia humanitatis

PUBLISHER, PRINTER AND DISTRIBUTOR
José Porrúa Turanzas, S. A.
Cea Bermúdez, 10 - Madrid-3
España

© *ANN BUGLIANI*

Dep. legal: M. 30.132.-1977

I. S. B. N. 84-7317-062-8

IMPRESO EN ESPAÑA
PRINTED IN SPAIN

Ediciones José Porrúa Turanzas, S. A.
Cea Bermúdez, 10 - Madrid-3

TALLERES GRÁFICOS PORRÚA, S. A.
JOSÉ, 10 - MADRID-29

To my parents,
Ana and César A. González

TABLE OF CONTENTS

PSYCHOMACHIE

CHAPTER I

THE FEMININE QUATERNION:
SOPHIA, MARY, THE CHURCH
AND THE SOUL

During his interviews with Jean Amrouche in 1951, Paul Claudel states that, for him, woman always represents four things: either the soul, the Church, the Virgin Mary, or Divine Wisdom, «*la Sagesse sacrée*» (1). Assertions of a similar nature date back as far as 1891 when Claudel, in a letter to Albert Mockel, explained that the Princess in *Tête d'Or* represents the soul, woman, Wisdom, and Piety (*T*, II, 1245). Apparently, for Claudel, all women—whether they be creatures of the creative imagination or not—are contained in this four-part frame of reference.

I would like to begin my study of women and the feminine principle in Claudel's works with an analysis of this four-

---

(1) Paul Claudel, *Mémoires improvisés* (Paris: Gallimard, 1969), p. 63. This source is henceforth cited in the text as *Mi*. References in the text to *T* indicate Claudel's *Théâtre*, eds. Jacques Madaule and Jacques Petit, Bibliothèque de la Pléiade, 2 vols. (Paris: Gallimard, 1965-1967), *J* refers to Claudel's *Journal*, eds. François Varillon and Jacques Petit, Bibliothèque de la Pléiade, 2 vols. (Paris: Gallimard, 1968-1969), *Opo* represents Claudel's *Oeuvre Poétique*, ed. Jacques Petit, Bibliothèque de la Pléiade (Paris: Gallimard, 1967), *Opr* stands for Claudel's *Oeuvres en Prose*, eds. Jacques Petit and Charles Galpérine, Bibliothèque de la Pléiade (Paris: Gallimard, 1965), and *Oc* indicates Claudel's *Oeuvres complètes*, 26 vols. (Paris: Gallimard, 1950-1967).

sided analogy, using Wisdom or Sophia as my starting point. I choose to begin with Sophia for two reasons. First, because Wisdom undoubtedly represents the loftiest valuation of femininity in both the western and eastern Judeo-Christian world. And second, because Claudel's discovery of Sophia dates all the way back to his conversion.

Sophia

As is commonly known, on the evening of December 25, 1886 Claudel had a religious experience in Notre Dame Cathedral which was to transform his life. On returning home that night he opened a Protestant Bible which had been given to his sister Camille by a friend, and read two passages. One dealt with the Apostles' encounter at Emmaus and the other was from the book of Proverbs, Chapter 8. It is this second passage which concerns us, for it is here that Sophia is described.

Sophia tells us that she was the first to be conceived —before the creation. She is full of joy and delight: «Je me délectais de chaque jour l'un après l'autre, en jouant sans cesse devant Lui, me jouant sur le globe de la terre» (2). (This trait naturally brings to mind characters such as Doña Musique.) Claudel often associates and/or identifies Sophia with Grace. Most important, however, is her creative function. She says: «Et moi j'étais avec Lui composant et conférent toutes choses» (3). Claudel calls her an incomparable mother and we learn that she is intimately connected with spiritual transformation and rebirth. He adds that it was her eyes «qui ont dérangé la Trinité elle-même, et L'ont invitée à créer le monde» (Oc, XXI, 175). Elsewhere he actually states that Divine Wisdom occupies in all things the position of principle and cause (Oc, XX, 315) and that it was Wisdom that created man and the world (T, II, 1512).

---

(2) Proverbs 8: 30-31.
(3) Ibid.

Statements of this nature, which attribute such an exalted role to Sophia, inevitably lead us to wonder what Claudel's attitude may have been on an important historical question —i.e., the possibility of the feminine principle existing within the Godhead itself.

Carl Jung tells us that the feminine principle was attributed to the Holy Ghost, who was called Sophia-Sapientia, by certain early Christians (4). In keeping with this, we also learn from Jung that the dove, which is a symbol of the Holy Ghost, was called Sophia and thought of as feminine (5). Although this view was later rejected by the Church, we still find elements in Claudel which are reminiscent of this early belief. He tells us that wisdom lives within us. She penetrates everywhere. He emphasizes her pneumatic nature by comparing her to the north wind, which brings to mind the fact that in the writings of the Church Fathers the south wind is an allegory of the Holy Ghost. In *L'Histoire de Tobie et de Sara* we are told by Azarius that Sara, who describes herself as «l'Aurore et cette espèce de Sagesse qui le précède» (*T*, II, 1311), was present at the creation as a bird who sang. Lala, who Claudel tells us is a figure of Sophia, compares herself to a bird one hears without seeing. Musique has a birthmark in the form of a dove beneath her shoulder. And finally, the Princess is nailed to a tree like a bird of the night. These and other passages seem to link or identify elements characterizing the Holy Ghost with Sophia, who is represented by Claudel's female characters.

Jung also points out that Sophia shares certain essential qualities with the Johannine Logos (6). We find a reflection of this too in Claudel:

---

(4) Carl G. Jung, *Psychology and Religion* (New Haven: Yale University Press, 1938), p. 89.
(5) Carl G. Jung, *Contributions to Analytical Psychology* (London: Kegan Paul, Trench, Trubner & Co. Ltd., and New York: Harcourt, Brace and Company, 1928), p. 115.
(6) Carl G. Jung, *Answer to Job*, trans. by R. F. C. Hull (London: Routledge & Kegan Paul Ltd., 1954), p. 39.

La voici donc au seuil de ma maison, la Parole qui
est comme une jeune fille éternelle!
Ouvre la porte! et la Sagesse de Dieu est devant
toi comme une tour de gloire et comme une reine
couronnée! (*Opo*, 248).

In *La Sagesse ou la parabole du festin* we are told that Sophia
is the Way. We see her «toute revêtue de chemins!» and
«toute habillée d'écriture». She gives herself to us and we
are told: «Prenez! Mangez! Buvez! Vivez!» (*T*, II, 1206-07).
Here she is obviously identified with Christ, the Word,
who also said He was the Way and of whose flesh and
blood we are invited to partake. Finally, in «Introduction
à un poème sur Dante» we are informed that eternal Wisdom
made herself flesh and only addressed us in parables (*Opr*,
427-28).

All this obviously points to the fact that there existed
in Claudel's mind an identification between the Godhead
and the feminine principle. But for a really clear statement
of Claudel's opinion regarding the possible bisexuality of
God we must turn to his *Journal*. In a passage written in
December 1942 he discusses St. Gregory of Nysse's theory
regarding the creation of man. St. Gregory postulates a
double creation. Troubled by the passage—«Dieu créa
l'homme à Son image: à l'image de Dieu Il le créa: mâle et
femelle Il le créa» (7)—he theorizes that God must first
have created man in His image—apparently asexual—and
then, after that, He must have created Adam. For God is
not male and female. Claudel retorts: Can we be sure of
that? Isn't woman an image of God in her own way, like
man? He then proceeds to give proof that there is something

---

(7) Genesis 1:27. It is interesting to note that the version of
this text Claudel used is far more provocative than any of the
versions I was able to locate. The English text I consulted, which
corresponds to all the French, Spanish, and Italian texts examined
by me, states: «So God created man in his own image, in the
image of God created he him; male and female created he *them*»
[italics mine].

feminine in God. He mentions Sophia and also passages in which God compares Himself to a mother.

The problem of Sophia's relation to God and her apparent identification with the Holy Ghost and Christ can be elucidated to some extent if we consider the fact that there are more than one Sophia. Claudel speaks of *La Sagesse divine, la Sagesse éternelle, la Sagesse incréée, la Sagesse incarnée,* and *la Sagesse créée.* The first three terms would seem to refer to the Sophia of Proverbs, Chapter 8, who was not created but conceived and seems to be co-eternal with the Godhead. The fourth term—*la Sagesse incarnée*—apparently refers to Christ. He appears to be the incarnation of *La Sagesse éternelle.* Finally, the fifth term—*la Sagesse créée*—is always associated with Mary. We learn from Ernest Beaumont's article on Sophia that all of this is more or less in keeping with sophiological thinking which postulates two Sophias: uncreated Wisdom or divine Sophia and created Wisdom or creaturely Sophia. Christ manifests the hypostatic image of uncreated Wisdom and Mary is the created hypostatis of created Wisdom (8).

With that we come to an understanding of the relationship between the first two terms of the quaternion Wisdom, Mary, the Church, and the soul. We can begin to grasp how these Claudelian analogies were conceived. I would now like to continue with an examination of what Mary came to mean to Claudel and how she affected his conception of womanhood.

Mary

Claudel tells us that it did not take him long to recognize the connection between Sophia and Mary. Just how long it did take, however, is a question which invites speculation.

_____
(8) Ernest Beaumont, «Claudel and Sophia», in *Claudel: A Reappraisal*, ed. Richard Griffiths (Chester Springs, Pa.: Dufour Editions, 1968), p. 94.

Claudel undoubtedly knew that the text from Proverbs regarding Sophia is the one read in the Catholic Church for the Feast of the Immaculate Conception, yet in his first statement concerning what women symbolize for him he omits mention of Mary. As noted above, in 1891 he stated that the Princess in *Tête d'Or* represents the soul, woman, Wisdom and Piety. Ernest Beaumont points out that the first evidence of the identification between Mary and Sophia having taken place appears in the poem «Chant de marche de Noël» which was first published in 1913 and is included in *Corona Benignitatis Anni Dei* (9). Here Claudel addresses Mary in terms which clearly indicate that he ascribes Sophian characteristics and functions to her. It would appear that this poem was written in 1911, the year in which he completed *L'Annonce faite à Marie* which is also imbued with a Marian spirit. It seems reasonable to assume, however, that Claudel identified Mary with Sophia in his own mind at an even earlier date. I feel that his devotion to Mary probably began to develop between 1904, when he was abandoned by Rosalie L., his mistress, and 1907 when he wrote *Magnificat* which is the first of his published works to be Marian in inspiration. Agnes Meyer, the friend in whom he confided the most, tells us:

> The futility of R's life and travels taught C. that one cannot run away from oneself, that the self must be faced and having in him so much purity, passion, force (brutal force even) so much need of compassion and love in his great lonelines, he sought and found all in the mother, the all embracing, all protecting arms of the Madonna (10).

In *La Rose et le rosaire* Claudel, while discussing the Assumption, states without any equivocation whatsoever that

(9) Ibid., p. 98.
(10) Agnes Meyer, «Note-Book», in *Claudel et l'Amérique II*, ed. Eugène Roberto, Cahier canadien Claudel 6 (Ottawa: Éditions de l'Université d'Ottawa, 1969), p. 186.

he repudiates the view of those who attribute undue power to Mary. He goes on to say that Mary is only a creature whose glory it is to serve. She is not Wisdom; she is only clothed in Wisdom (*Oc*, XXI, 248). It must be noted, however, that the thrust of most of his remarks concerning Mary belies this standpoint. In «Chant de marche de Noël», cited above, he affirms that it was the Virgin's face that the Almighty had placed before Him at the creation. It was she who made the light shine forth. Elsewhere he tells us: «Au Livre des Proverbes on voit l'idée de la Vierge future servant de provocation à toute la création physique» (*Oc*, XXV, 518). He also claims that the image of the Holy Virgin served «de thème et de proposition à la commençante modulation de l'univers» (*Oc*, XXV, 536). Finally, he asserts that it is of Mary that God has thought through all eternity and that it is for her that He created the world (*Oc*, XXV, 532).

It seems abundantly clear that in these passages Claudel has fully identified Mary with Wisdom and not only with created Wisdom but also with uncreated Wisdom. She seems almost to introduce a fourth term into the Godhead. There are things, we are told, which Christ understands only if His mother whispers them to Him (*Oc*, XXI, 213). She has shown herself to be stronger than He. She was charged with capturing His eternity in the net of time and she acquainted Him with death (*Oc*, XXV, 514). Her face destroys darkness and death (*Oc*, XXI, 206). Claudel calls her Our August Sovereign and rebukes Péguy for having had too lowly a conception of her. He also chides Dante for having committed a grave theological error by placing her merely a little higher than the other saints in his *Paradise*. He explains that it is not Mary who is in paradise, but paradise which is wholly confirmed by Mary. For Claudel, she is co-redemptrice of humanity. Toward the end of his life he would only dare to address her in prayer as «Madame».

It should, however, be noted that Claudel's attitude regarding Mary seems to waver and is at times contradictory.

I have already presented one example of this above. To illustrate the point further I will briefly discuss one of the symbols associated with Mary (and also with Sophia)—the moon, which is often linked with the mirror image. Mary is said to be the perfect moon. Her function is to reveal the One she loves from whom she cannot turn her face. As the moon derives its light from the sun and then transmits it to earth, so it is with Mary who draws her brilliance from her Son. She is the woman clothed in the sun which is mentioned in the Apocalypse. She offers no obstacles to His will and is therefore full of Grace. She is the perfect void which allows His action to work through her. As the moon presides over the waters so she presides over everything in us which is liquid and capable of desire and reflection. Every morning she brings to the feet of her Son the tide of souls. She gives God to humanity and humanity to God. In analogous terms he likens her to a mirror—a mirror without blemish in which we see God and in which we also see ourselves as we really are. Her function then is both active and passive. As a mirror she passively receives and conserves an image. Her active role is to show and communicate the image received to all the other mirrors which are turned towards her. (These other mirrors are our souls.) Is she then merely a reflection? Does she only transmit? One would be tempted to conclude as much from the above. But Claudel says no, and herein lies the contradiction. He tells us she is also a source. Is she merely a servant? Claudel says yes, but her mode of service is maternal. «Sa manière de service est d'être mère, et, servante parfaite, d'être une mère parfaite» (Oc, XXI, 427). And although he says that the essence of service is administrative and not creative, one might well ask what could be more creative than the maternal function.

Of prime importance, of course, is the fact that Mary is the mother of Christ. Claudel is careful to note that this maternal relationship was not limited to the nine months of pregnancy. Her Son is not a statue which the sculptor abandons once the work is done. On the contrary, everywhere He goes she is with Him as mother. «Son coeur dans une telle donation ne cesse pas d'être l'ouvrier du Sien, et, de l'un à l'autre, la vie tour à tour donnée et reçue ne cesse pas de circuler» (*Oc, XXV, 524*). And just as Mary is the mother of Christ, she is also said to be our spiritual mother. When in later life Claudel thinks back on his conversion, on his spiritual rebirth, he attributes it to the workings of Mary, identifying her with Sophia whose creative function she has assumed. Just as Sophia is said to be in rapport with what is «oval» in man's heart («oval» connoting egg, seed, etc.), Mary is said to have a seminal vocation. She cooperates with that germ of God within us so that we might be born again, so that someone in His image might come to life. Claudel says that she remakes us both inwardly and outwardly. She is the woman who John saw giving birth in the sun—to the sun, adds Claudel. Her birth pains never cease for she never stops giving birth to Christ, and Christ in us.

This creative function also operates in a different but analogous way. Wisdom was called daughter of the wind, «fille du souffle». (The word «*souffle*» is almost always associated with creativity and inspiration in Claudel's work.) As Mary and Sophia merge, Mary—who assumes her functions—becomes the inspired Virgin. Thus a new dimension is added to her maternity and to her creativity. She was the one to give breath (*souffle*) and speech (*parole*) to her Son and likewise it is now she who inspires the artist. «Elle sème d'idées le papier des écrivains» (*Oc, XXI, 206*).

It must also be pointed out that in addition to being mother, Mary is the spiritual bride and wife of Christ. In this role she finds expression through the lips of the Shulamite —the bride or fiancée from the Song of Solomon. This canticle is accepted by the Church as being an allegory describing the relationship between the *Sponsa* and *Sponsus,* i.e., Mary and Christ. It is in this book that are found many of the symbol-attributes associated with the Virgin. Some of the attributes ascribed to the Virgin in the Litany of Loretto can also be traced back to the Song of Songs. For us the most important of the symbols from Solomon's book—those elaborated on by Claudel—are: the sun, the rose (11) and the lily (the lily among thorns), myrrh, the vine, the fruit (the pomegranate), milk and wine, the enclosed garden and the sealed fountain, the tower or wall, the door, the veil, the dove, and the vessel or goblet. From the Lorettian Litany we should mention the house of gold and the morning star. Claudel also associates Mary with the ocean, with the star of the ocean, and, as we have seen, with the moon and with mirrors.

The Song of Songs is of course a love poem, perhaps a wedding song. Early mystical interpreters of the Canticle saw the bride as Israel and the Bridegroom as Yahweh. Claudel in his commentary of the book interprets the bride as being not only Mary, but also the Church and the soul. This being the case, we can now tie in all the figures discussed thus far, for Sophia is also said to be the bride of God.

Those who have not been able to perceive or understand the spiritual symbolism of the Song have always objected to its eroticism. Similarly, many have been struck by the erotic nature of Claudel's spirituality. Agnes Meyer, who was a Protestant, felt that the voluptuousness of Claudel's religious concepts was staggering. It is, I believe, important to understand that this voluptuousness or eroticism is completely in keeping with certain currents in Church tradition. (One need only think of medieval mysticism— Mechtild von Magdeburg, for example; or the Spanish mystics: Fray Luis de León, Santa Teresa de Ávila, and San Juan de la Cruz.) This Christian eroticism, which is often perfectly frank, has always found its inspiration in the Song of Solomon. The Church Fathers explicitly accepted the unmistakably erotic nature of some of

---

(11) Contrary to what Jacqueline de Labriolle says in her article, «Le Thème de la Rose» (*La Revue des Lettres Modernes*, Nos. 134-136 [1966], 93), this image does appear in the Canticle. The Shulamite says that she is the rose of Sharon (Song 2:1).

the symbol-attributes of the Virgin stemming from the Canticle. St. Ambrosius interprets the *hortus conclusus* (enclosed garden) as virginity and for St. Augustine, Mary is the bridal chamber, i.e., the virginal womb.

Before going on to a discussion of my next topic—the Church, I would like to mention that Claudel's feminine characters are frequently associated with the fiancée from the Song of Solomon. There is Violaine, of course. The love scene between her and Jacques in Act II of *L'Annonce faite à Marie* is particularly evocative. The decor (a kind of garden with a fountain) and the language («O ma fiancée à travers les branches en fleurs, salut!» [*T*, II, 167] parallel those found in the Canticle. In *Le Père humilié* we find another garden scene. Here, though, the association is more obvious and eventually Sichel actually tells her daughter that she sounds like Solomon's bride. Finally, the scene of the encounter between Musique and the Viceroy has elements which are reminiscent of the atmosphere which characterizes the Canticle.

The Church

It is not too difficult to understand the relationship between Sophia and Mary. It is, however, less apparent and more difficult to grasp how and why Sophia/Mary is associated with the Church. It must be noted, to begin with, that the Church may be considered on two levels. It may be considered as a building, a structure; or as an organism, i.e., the body of Christ. As a building or structure the Church is likened to the maternal womb. Its cupola is compared to an egg and in its center lies «la semence eucharistique» or host. We know that Claudel's conversion took place in Notre Dame Cathedral and he speaks of that church as being «une espèce de couveuse» (*J*, I, 644). It is in the cavity of the church that spiritual rebirth takes place. The church is then in the fullest sense a mother and it is through this function that she is identified with Mary and Sophia. She then, like

— 11 —

Mary, also never ceases to give birth to the Sons of God who are a temporal continuation of Christ Himself. The sun-woman seen by John who was travailed with birth pains is also the Church.

To this cavity which is the church are ascribed all the characteristics typifying a womb. In the ceremony known in the Catholic Church as *benedictio fontis*, the baptismal font is actually spoken of as «immaculatis divini fontis uterus» (the immaculate womb of the divine fountain-head). Here the church is the Bride and Mother and the baptismal font is her womb, but for Claudel the entire church interior is considered to be «le ventre maternel». It is called «la coque du vide seminal» (*T, I, 653*). The liquid typifying the amniotic fluid is present throughout the church in the form of glass. Claudel also speaks of «le bain de ténèbres bienfaisantes» (*Opr, 136*). When in Notre Dame he compares himself to the prophet Jeremiah buried in his cistern (*Opo, 216*). It is through this darkness and liquidity that we are able to resume contact with our original nothingness. The darkness into which we disappear brings us closer to God. He speaks of «l'obscurissement et la sécurité de son gouffre tutélaire» (*Opo, 216*) and of the eternal shadows (recalling the overshadowing of Mary) that melt the envelope of our personal darkness. He would like to see a church built «sur l'ombre même en tant que matériau essentiel» (*Opr, 136*) as Pierre was to do in *L'Annonce faite à Marie*. This darkness or night is also compared to that of the tomb for it must not be forgotten that, like Christ, we must die before we can be born again. The site of the sacrifice is the altar where the holocaust takes place. In keeping with this, the Cathedral of le Mans is compared to Jonah's whale, seen from the inside, which brings to mind the fact that the story of Jonah and the whale is considered to be an allegory of Christ's death and resurrection.

The symbolism uniting the Shulamite, Sophia/Mary, and the Church is often complex. To illustrate this point I will briefly discuss the flower symbols connected with these figures.

— 12 —

The bride in the Song of Solomon tells us that she is the rose of Sharon and the lily of the Valleys. In the Litany of Loretto the rose is called the pure womb that blossoms and is associated with Mary. The womb, of course, is also the Church. Claudel has the bride of the Canticle say: «Je suis tous ces lys ensemble qui ne font qu'une seule tige en une corolle suprême où l'Esprit Saint ne cessera de S'approvisioner de pollen» (*Oc,* XXII, 248) which would seem to indicate that he too has made the identification—bride/Mary/Church/rose or lily.

The Church is also likened to a city. Just as a city is made of stones, so too the Church. But she is made both of stone building-blocks and of living stones. She is built upon the rock that gave Peter his name. On a concrete level the relationship between the Church and the city is readily apparent. As Claudel points out, the city was born around the church, of the church. On a symbolic level, it is with the new Jerusalem that the Church is usually compared and in this context she is again identified with Sophia and Mary. John tells us in the Apocalypse that he saw the holy city new Jerusalem coming down from God out of heaven, prepared as a bride adorned for her husband. Here the identification is made with the Shulamite and Mary. Wisdom comes into the picture through her association with the «crossroads» image which is connected with both the city and the Church. The Church, Claudel tells us, is a solidification of the crossroads which is symbolic of the cross (*Opr,* 263). We subsequently learn that Sophia loves the crossroads. The church then is a prototype of Wisdom—her position is at the crossroads. The Princess in *Tête d'Or,* who we know symbolizes Wisdom, says: «Je me tiens au carrefour des chemins, et, dans les villes mêmes» (*T,* I, 65). Finally, we see that Lala in *La Ville,* who also represents Sophia, is connected with the founding of the new city.

As mentioned above, the Church, which is made up of living stones, is also called the body of Christ. Despite the apparent contradiction, the Church does not lose her feminine nature even though she is called the body of Christ. This for two reasons. First, because Christ's flesh came wholly from Mary and second, because Christ's body is ascribed a maternal function in connection with the Church. It is said that the Church was born out of the wound Christ received beneath his heart when he was on the cross. This being the case, we see that the birth of the Church parallels the birth of Eve—it was prefigured by the birth of Eve. And just as Eve becomes Adam's bride, so the Church becomes the bride of Christ. Pierre de Craon in *L'Annonce faite à Marie*, who is called the father of his churches, says: «Cette église seule sera ma femme qui va être tirée de mon côté comme une Ève de pierre, dans le sommeil de la douleur» (*T*, II, 144).

On a broader scale we can now see a series of events which correspond one to the other. God conceives Sophia; Adam gives birth to Eve; and Christ engenders the Church. The Church is identified with Mary and the new city and the bridal role is ascribed to all five of these feminine proto-types, in keeping with the relationship between Adam and Eve. Finally, the three masculine entities are considered to have an underlying female principle which has enabled them to carry out the maternal function that is essentially feminine. For an understanding of how this female principle characterizes itself on the human level, we must further investigate the story of Adam and Eve. This will serve as introduction to a discussion of the soul, the last element of our feminine quaternion.

The Soul

Through the female figures discussed thus far—Sophia and Mary—we have seen womanhood exalted to almost unimagined heights. Man is truly born of woman for although Eve was taken from Adam's side, it was to Sophia that Adam owed his creation. Furthermore, Eve's birth can be said to have been a sort of immaculate conception since she was not made of clay as Adam was. And although it was she who first succumbed to temptation, it was also through her that mankind was redeemed. She was the depository of the promised salvation. In his treatment of the creation of Eve, Claudel points out that her birth can be considered as the extrication, the removal from Adam of a feminine principle already existing in him. This idea stems from the Biblical passage, already cited above, in which we are told that God created man in his image, i.e., male and female. As we have seen, Claudel drew from this text his theory on the bisexuality of God. Now we see that on the strength of this text he also concludes that to be in the image of God man must also have this double nature. Eve's birth can be compared to the removal of a tree, the roots of which are left behind. In other words, something feminine persists in the male —something whose existence is felt because of and through its absence. Man has been left with a feminine void within him and it is this feminine void which we are told is his soul.

In discussing the soul, Claudel frequently compares it to a vase—a Chinese vase whose essence it is to be empty. The Chinese vase is said to be the supreme exhalation of the profound lotus, the sacred globe which opens, the receptacle of the soul that flowers and offers its nothingness (*Opr,* 785). All of this is of course reminiscent of taoist thinking and terminology. Claudel admits that the tao had a great influence on him. He characterizes it as a kind of glorification of nothingness or the void, a recommendation that man always keep himself in a state of perfect availability (*disponibilité*) (*Mi,* 174). He quotes Lao Tze as saying that emptiness is the mystic way in all things, the tao, the soul, the tendency —it is the measured aspiration to which the vase gives most perfect form (*Opr,* 892). We also learn that this emptiness or void is by its very essence feminine. Yin, the feminine principle in Chinese thought, is dark and empty; whereas yang, the masculine principle, is light and full.

Drawing from another culture, the Indian culture, Claudel considers an analogous concept in his discussion of the yoni. In Shaktism, which is the cult of Shakti, the wife of Shiva, one of the Hindu gods, the yoni is the female principle, i.e., the external female genitals regarded as a symbol of Shakti. Claudel associates this female principle—the yoni—with the egg, the seed, and the zero (*J*, I, 19). Elsewhere the zero or O is associated with the soul (*J*, I, 848) and with woman (*Opr*, 82).

The question which inevitably arises at this point is: What of woman's soul? As we consider this longstanding belief in the femininity of the soul, we can better understand the scholastic question formulated during the ecclesiastical Middle Ages: *Habet mulier animam?* Does woman have a soul, and if so, is it feminine? If we take into account Claudel's theory on the bisexuality of each individual, then our answer to the second question must of needs be no—her soul is probably not feminine. We know that Jung counterbalances his theory regarding the feminine principle in man, which he calls Anima, by positing the existence of a masculine principle in woman, which he calls Animus. Although Claudel's concept of Anima is amazingly close to Jung's, we find no mention in Claudel's prose or poetry of Animus in the Jungian sense. (Claudel's Animus is something quite different.) Yet, despite this apparent lacuna, the notion that there exists a masculine principle in woman is definitely present in Claudel's theatre. We need only think of Ysé, who says when speaking of her husband: «Je suis un homme! Je l'aime comme on aime une femme» (*T*, I, 1006). Also interesting is the frequency with which we see Claudel's heroines dressed as men. Lumîr, Prouhèze, Sept-Épées, la Bouchère, and Jeanne d'Arc all have occasion to disguise themselves as men. We also know that several of his women—Lumîr, Prouhèze, Sept-Épées, and Jeanne d'Arc—have fought as soldiers. We see then that this principle of bisexuality completely permeates Claudels thought and is applicable to both men and women. It is also interesting to note that this theory corresponds on a psychic or spiritual level to what we know to be true on the physical plane. Jung points out that the Anima is probably «a psychical representation of the minority of female genes in a male body» (12). This assumption becomes all the more likely, he adds, when we consider that the same Anima figure «is not to be found in the imagery of a feminine unconscious» (13).

I would like to move on now to consider the ways in which Claudel associates or identifies the soul with the various feminine figures discussed thus far. I choose again to begin with Sophia as I believe her identification with the soul has perhaps the most interesting consequences.

In a letter written to Francis Jammes in 1900 Claudel states: «Toute sensation à laquelle elle n'a point sa part contriste en nous la Sagesse qui est toujours là comme une femme insupportable» (14). It would seem that in this statement Claudel has identified Sophia with the soul which is elsewhere spoken of as being an intolerable woman living within him. That being the case, he will now ascribe all the Sophian characteristics and functions to the soul. Most important, we learn that because of this shared nature our souls were actually present at the creation through Sophia. «Quand Il composait l'Univers, quand Il disposait avec beauté le Jeu, quand Il déclenchait l'énorme cérémonie, / Quelque chose de nous avec lui, voyant tout, se réjouissait dans son oeuvre» (*Opo*, 230). Our souls then somehow participate in the eternity of God and are, as André Vachon points out, literally anterior to death (15).

This same passage also serves to call to mind another Sophian attribute mentioned previously—Sapientia is a joyous creature, a playful creature. I have already pointed out how Doña Musique is Sophian in this sense. Now I can add that the soul also is said to share this quality—a quality which is

---

(12) Jung, *Psychology and Religion*, p. 34.
(13) Ibid.
(14) Paul Claudel, Francis Jammes, and Gabriel Frizeau, *Correspondance 1897-1938* (Paris: Gallimard, 1952), p. 29.
(15) André Vachon, *Le Temps et l'espace dans l'oeuvre de Paul Claudel* (Paris: Éditions du Seuil, 1965), p. 152.

2

essentially musical in nature. Sara in *L'Histoire de Tobie et de Sara,* who represents the human soul, is compared to a singing bird. Claudel, borrowing from Ecclesiasticus, calls the soul the daughter of song. He likens her to a musical instrument. Connected with this is another important attribute of Wisdom which is now also imputed to the soul—her pneumatic nature, already discussed above. Claudel calls his soul «*moi* en tant que centre d'aspiration» (*Opr,* 93). The soul is said to breathe. Returning for a moment to the Chinese vase Claudel describes in *Ægri Somnia* we might mention that he calls it «l'âme en silence qui célèbre son opération» and subsequently adds that it is «le souffle en acte» (*Opr,* 893). Anima then, as her name denotes (anima < *anemos* = wind), is a breath-being. Another interesting point is her frequent association with fire—namely, our internal combustion. This brings to mind the Holy Ghost, with whom Sophia also shares some attributes, who is symbolized by the wind and tongues of fire.

The soul is also compared to a city and a people. The city with which she is usually connected is Celestial Jerusalem. This linking takes place most frequently through use of the pearl image. The pearl, pure and eternal, is the image of the redeemed soul and as such serves as door to the mystic Jerusalem. Sara, who we know represents the soul, is compared to a besieged city.

The comparison of the soul with a people is obviously connected with the city image, but it also leads us in another direction—to the association of the soul with the Church. In a passage from *Magnificat* Claudel compares his soul to a forest or a people of murmuring voices (*Opo,* 256). Elsewhere mention is made of the «temple des arbres» (*T,* I, 32). This connects the soul to the Church by way of the image «a people» which is associated with forests and trees, i.e., temple symbols.

Other, less circuitous, associations can of course also be made between the soul and the Church. In fact, the two most important characteristics of the church interior which were discussed above—darkness and liquidity—are also attributes of the soul. Darkness and shadows are the soul's elements. In addition, two types of liquids are associated with her—water and blood. Often, the soul is actually said to be liquid. It is called «cette sève essentielle, cette humidité intérieure» (*T*, I, 183). In *L'Esprit et l'eau* we find mention made of a phenomenon that can only be called the liquefaction of the soul. We see here a process of spiritual maturation in the poet which has as its product the distillation of a drop of water from his soul (*Opo*, 244-45). In *L'Oeil écoute* we are told that water and the soul are in alliance—an alliance which is formed at baptism (*Opr*, 326). Concerning the blood we learn that it is the servant and worker of the soul, the support of the soul. These two elements, water and blood, combined with shadows and mention of the baptismal rite, all bring to mind the birth of the Church from Christ's wound (which secreted blood and water) and also our previous discussion of the Church as womb. It is quite apparent, I believe, that to really be in the image of Sophia, the Church, or Mary, the human soul must have a creative function. We now begin to see that she, in Claudel's view, has been fashioned after a womb and consequently is destined to fulfill a maternal role. (At this point we can better understand his use of the vase image and his discussion of the yoni with which he associates the egg, seed, and zero.)

Our soul is called the mother cell, the essential cell which is the principle of our movements and our affections. She is «cela par quoi le corps humain est ce qu'il est, son acte, sa semence continuellement opérante» (*Opo*, 106). Once wounded and thereby made fecund, she has the power to solidify time into eternity, to produce the essential pearl, to transform us into the Sons of God, to give birth to Christ in us so that once again the Word may become flesh (16). The

---

(16) Eugène Roberto discusses the rebirth process and the transformation of the soul in a fascinating study, «*Le Jet de pierre*» (*Formes et figures*, Cahier canadien Claudel 5 [Ottawa: Éditions de l'Université d'Ottawa, 1967], pp. 75-96).

fecundation takes place through the power of the Holy Spirit and the Word. So it may be said that our spiritual rebirth in every way parallels the birth of Christ. That is why Claudel calls the soul «cette autre Marie» and why he attributes to her—in her redeemed state—all the Marian attributes. Like Mary, in addition to being mother she is also chaste bride. (Sara as symbol of the soul is the bride of Christ, personified in Tobie.) Like the Shulamite she is black but beautiful—«la Marie noire». The soul is servant, guide, conductor, and source of inspiration. She is identified with stars and the moon, with the vase, as mentioned above, and with an enclosed garden. She is called a fruit and a vine. She is said to be a mirror and is referred to as a wall. Finally, the soul is likened to the circular rose which welcomes the pollen of divine Grace and whose very essence, in keeping with her pneumatic nature, is the perfume she exhales.

Now that I have described the salient characteristics of the redeemed soul, the question remains: What of the unredeemed soul? What of the soul in its natural state? On a broader plane, we might even ask—keeping in mind that the soul along with Mary, the Church and Sophia are representative of women—whether Claudel's exalted vision of women isn't counterbalanced by a negative valuation at the opposite end of the scale. In fact, we intuitively sense that this must be the case. We know that many of the symbols and images discussed thus far have their negative counterparts. Celestial Jerusalem is contrasted with Babylon the Mother of Harlots in the Bible. The chaste bride is in contradistinction to the faithless wife. The moon has its dark underside as do mirrors. We also know that it is only through discussion of the soul that any negative aspects could enter into Claudel's feminine quaternion.

There is a woman within, we learn, who is blind and completely black. This woman within has been disfigured by our internal night. (We see now that this inner darkness has both a positive and negative potential. It can become the very instrument of the soul's transformation. It can furnish her with form and nourishment. Or, it can harm her. Claudel speaks of «la grande flamme noire de l'âme qui brûle de toutes parts comme une cité dévorée!» [T, I, 1027]). A character such as Jobarbara in *Le Soulier de satin* seems to embody, on a rather harmless level, many of the traits of the dark soul. She is, of course, pagan, but above all she is black and says that she shines like a mirror, which puts us in mind of Mary. Pensée in *Le Père humilié* might also be mentioned since she, because of her physical and spiritual blindness, is enveloped in darkness. This is obviously not to imply that Mary in any way participates in negative aspects or functions. It is true that Claudel says she has incorporated herself into our darkness, yet she is present there primarily as a potential function. It is clear that Claudel feels the soul, regardless of how debased she may become, never loses her regenerative potentiality.

In the original version of the parable of Animus and Anima appearing in Claudel's *Journal* Animus, who represents the mind or intellect, subjugates Anima, the soul, by actually making a prisoner of her (T, I, 652). Elsewhere, Claudel refers to his soul as «la séquestrée», his forgotten sister who has been locked in a deep cellar full of spiders and rats (Oc, XXIII, 36). We are also told that both Lumîr and Pensée are symbolic of the incarcerated soul, the soul which has been exiled. In the parable Anima, despite the ill-treatment received, is still able to function. She retains her spirituality and seems eager to be united with her divine lover. This is in contrast with the picture we get in other texts. In «L'Art et la Foi» Anima is called «cette Furie séquestrée» (Opr, 66) and in one of the *Conversations dans le Loir-et-Cher* we see that when Anima's prison is opened she refuses to come out. She is called «notre larve sans visage» and is compared to an animal who has grown used to its cage and will not leave it (Opr, 708). This comparison brings us close to another image Claudel uses to describe the soul—an image which is singularly revealing. The soul, in keeping with her pneumatic nature, is often compared to winged creatures—to doves, angels, and, on one occasion, to an eagle. But most important and most provocative is her association with the butterfly. The butterfly is said to be the palpitating symbol of the human soul. To understand what this implies for Claudel, we must reproduce here part of a speech made by Orian in *Le Père humilié:*

> Ainsi l'absurde papillon, cette chose palpitante et dégoûtante, le papillon qui n'est qu'un sale ver avec des ailes énormes, aussi inconsistant que de l'haleine,
> Et qui ne sait rien que de se jeter, de se rejeter, stupidement, et se jeter encore de toutes ses forces misérables
> Contre le globe de la lampe, et qui, quand il s'interrompt, est comme mort, quelque chose de rampant,
> Quelque chose d'immonde et de rampant que l'on ne saurait toucher (*T*, II, 543).

In keeping with this, elsewhere Claudel calls the soul «cette espèce d'ange à la fois et cette espèce de monstre» (*Opo,* 1001). The same naturally could be said of woman since the soul is in her image.

CHAPTER II

WOMAN AND THE LOVE
RELATIONSHIP

In his *Journal* Paul Claudel tells us: «Toute femme porte sur son visage le reflet de l'Immaculée conception» (*J*, II, 489). He adds in *La Rose et le rosaire* that the election of Mary has sanctified woman. These remarks point to Claudel's lofty assessment of womanhood. We know that women for him always represent either Sophia, Mary, the Church, or the soul—all exalted feminine figures. Yet, we have learned from our analysis of the soul in the preceeding chapter that Claudel's conception of womanhood is also characterized by highly negative valuations.

This ambivalent attitude is readily apparent in Claudel's work from the outset. The classic Claudelian syzygy with its positive and negative components makes its first appearance in *L'Endormie,* with the pair Strombo and Galaxaure. In *Tête d'Or,* the woman in the first act is to be contrasted with the Princess. Other such duos of course also exist—Mara and Violaine, Lechy and Marthe, Lumîr and Sichel, Brindosier and Hélène. On a different level, the ubiquitous syzygy is at times internalized and as a result, some of Claudel's characters carry this dual nature within them. Brindosier, for instance, like everyone else on the island of Naxos, is half beast and half god. The Moon, a female character in *L'Ours et la Lune,* seems also to suffer from a split personality. Both of these figures—the nymph (or *faunesse*) and the moon—appear frequently in Claudel's work and are reminiscent of the butterfly image discussed in Chapter I. They both remind us that for Claudel woman, like the soul, is half angel and half monster, half god and half beast, half light and half dark.

At this point we know that radiant, angelic femininity is undoubtedly Sophian or Marian in nature. We also know of Claudel's reverence for this aspect of womanhood. We do not know, however, what characterizes the dark side of woman—her earthly nature—or what the masculine reaction to this side of her is. Therefore, I would like to begin this chapter, in which I deal with the interaction between the sexes, by examining natural woman and man's assessment of her.

To begin with, Claudel tells us that woman is more earthbound than man. «La femme est plus près de la terre que vous autres et elle respire de plus près ses fumées» (*T, I,* 455). This quality is most important as it accounts for many of the male attitudes vis-à-vis woman. To a certain extent, for instance, it serves to explain the masculine feeling of superiority which is so pronounced in Claudel's universe. It helps us understand why Tête d'Or would call his wife «horreur vivante, honte, ignominie comblée de désirs» (*T, I,* 34), or why he would rank woman as one of the three major factors contributing to man's degradation.

In *Le Repos du septième jour* we learn that all flesh comes from woman: «La chair / Vient de la femme, et comme elle, elle est curieuse et lâche» (*T, I,* 822-23). This flesh is also said to be of a bestial nature. The fleshly and the earthly are of course two different sides of the same coin. Sin is said to flow from both just as naturally as life. Woman is then the font of both life and of sin, these two being intermingled at the source. (We know that in *Le Livre de Cristophe Colomb* Envy, Ignorance, Vanity, and Avarice are women—four grand ladies. Claudel also refers to Violence and Lust as women.) Woman carries and transmits the principle of mortality. As Claudel tells us: «La femme est là avec son corps et son coeur jaloux pour empêcher les hommes d'être des anges et pour maintenir les droits du péché originel» (*Opr,* 720). In *La Ville, le premier consacré* says: «Qu'est-ce que les femmes ont à dire? par qui nous avons lieu de mourir» (*T,* I, 410).

Woman's chthonic nature also implies other traits. Lala explains:

> La femme est plus près de la terre que vous autres et elle respire de plus près ses fumées.
> Et c'est ainsi qu'autrefois l'on dit
> Que l'esprit de Python l'emplissait et que la Prophetesse de Voleurs,
> Deux piques aux mains et barbouillée de sang de boeuf, dansant devant le feu de la marmite! (*T,* I, 455).

As we see in this passage, woman has certain susceptibilities that stem from her close contact with the elemental forces of nature. She exercises functions which transcend the limits of reason—that essentially masculine trait. As a result, she is viewed by man with suspicion.

Man finds her fanciful and capricious like Volpilla, Brindosier, or—on another level—Lechy who is said to represent «l'imagination un peu folle, qui entraîne le corps, qui le fait envoler» (*Mi,* 133). She also seems elusive. Lala warns: «Et que nul ne compte se saisir de moi et m'installer chez lui / Comme une vache qui lèche de la langue avec douceur le mur où elle est attachée» (*T,* I, 454). This characteristic is also present in Musique who admits: «Je veux le remplir tout à coup et le quitter instantanément [*T,* II, 709]. Or she may appear primitive and orgiastic like Thalie and Jobarbara. In Claudel's universe it is also she who is the seer and prophet. She is given to trances and at times receives sudden insights of mysterious origin. Thalie, for instance, was known to take leave of her senses on occasion. «Parfois / Un transport l'agite, ... C'est quand s'étend le soir que comme hors d'elle même, elle pousse des cris aigus!» (*T,* I, 329). Lala tells us she will be a prophet to the people and, as she lay dying, Tête d'Or's companion also claimed that she could prophesy. Lechy too is said to have a prophetic spirit and in this Claudel feels she resembles Cassandra. Jobarbara knows black magic. And finally, Ysé and Lumîr are both seen to receive strange revelations in a trance-like state. (This is also true of the Princess and Prouhèze. But here the accent is decidedly supernatural, whereas, in all the examples cited above, the trances, prophecies, and revelations are more chthonic in nature.)

It should perhaps be noted that in Claudel's theatre these powers hardly ever seem to be operative in the male characters. The highly charged masculine reaction to all of these phenomena is then not at all surprising. Woman seems to be the supreme mystery. Claudel tells us: «Mais n'est-ce pas sur le front de *La Femme* que l'Ange de l'Apocalypse nous fait lire le mot MYSTÈRE et quel mystère plus grand que la Femme en effet, virtuellement enceinte de tout ce qui est à venir, inconnue, inconnaissable, imprévisible? Quel emmagasinage de points d'interrogation?» (*Oc,* XXV, 483). (We should keep in mind at this point that the word MYSTERY appears on the forehead of the Harlot of Babylon in the Apocalypse. We are still on a very earthly level.) He adds that she is the possibility of something hidden, a secret being charged with meaning. She is as inexplicable as God Himself. Lechy says that woman arrives from the unknown; she is the door to the unknown; she *is* the unknown. She has the keys to the future. And this quality makes her seem all-knowing. To Mesa, Ysé is «quelqu'un qui dort et qui sait tout» (*T,* I, 1109).

Nearly all of Claudel's female characters are surrounded by an aura of mystery. They are often associated with the night like Pensée, or Ysé who compares herself to an animal that lives at night, or Lechy who disguises herself as a night butterfly. Most of them, at one point or other, are hidden behind veils. The veil image is a constant in Claudel's theatre. The Princess, Thalie, Lala, Violaine, Prouhèze, and Hélène all appear veiled. Pensée compares the night in which she is enveloped to a veil. And Claudel concludes that woman herself is a veil behind which much is hidden including the future.

This mysterious quality of woman leads to much confusion on the part of the male. As Ysé says: «Un homme, / Ça ne connaît pas plus sa femme que sa mère» (*T, I, 1017*). Tête d'Or admits: «Et elle me regardait et je n'ai pas su ce qu'elle voulait me dire. Qui est-ce qui comprend les femmes?» (*T, I, 175*). Then Claudel rather bitterly adds: «La femme ne *sort* jamais, n'est complètement elle-même qu'actrice» (*J, I, 233*). And we see that he has created two female characters of this profession—Lechy and the actress in *Le Soulier de satin*. Louis and Rodrigue, through lack of discernment, are both fooled by these women. In fact, we know that the men in Claudel's theatre are often duped by women because of this problem. We need only recall two examples which caricature the dilemma. In *L'Endormie* the poet serenades the hideous Strombo, thinking she is Galaxaure and in *Protée* Ménélas believes that the satyr is a beautiful nymph. Later he mistakes Brindosier for Hélène. In both cases the hero has been misled by a woman into misjudging another woman and in both instances masculine discernment has been completely lacking.

This point and other points touched on above inevitably lead us into our discussion of the interaction between the sexes. Therefore, as a means of furthering our understanding of woman's role in the Claudelian universe, let us now explore the love relationship as seen in Claudel's works.

I would like to begin by treating an aspect of this relationship which has received much critical attention: the phenomenon known as fascination or love at first sight. This theme runs all the way through Claudel's theatre. In *Fragment d'un drame* Marie calls her lover «mon jumeau» which suggests that they are kindred spirits somehow made for one another. The abruptness with which some of the ties in *La Ville* are formed suggests sudden, irresistible fascination. In *La Jeune Fille Violaine* (second version), Pierre mentions recognition when discussing his relationship with Violaine (*T*, I, 572) and Louis, in the first version of *L'Échange*, claims that all he had to do was take Marthe's hand for her to follow him at their first meeting (*T*, I, 687). From these examples we see that the theme of love at first sight was present in Claudel's theatre from the first.

It should be underscored, however, that after 1901, that is, following his encounter with Rosalie L., the theme became one of much greater moment. To illustrate this point we need only bring to mind the importance of the scene of recognition in Act I of *Partage de midi*, or recall how in Act II Mesa quite candidly admits: «J'ai frémi en te reconnaissant, et toute mon âme a cédé!» (*T*, I, 1110). For further evidence, the second version of *L'Échange*, written in 1951, might be contrasted with the first, written in 1893. The theme of the predestined lovers who recognize each other and fall in love on sight is much more fully developed in the second version of that play than in the first. In the 1951 text Louis actually says (although he contradicts himself later) that he and Marthe were made for each other (*T*, I, 734).

To cite other instances of the presence of this theme, we might add that in *L'Otage* Georges calls Sygne «mon étrange jumeau» (*T*, II, 227). In *Le Pain dur* Lumîr says to Louis: «Il y a tout de même en toi quelque chose qui me comprend et qui est mon frère!» (*T*, II, 473). And in *Le Père humilié* we find a scene of recognition which is reminiscent of the one in *Partage de midi*. *Le Père humilié* also contains many other allusions to this phenomenon. Finally, in *Soulier de satin* Rodrigue and Prouhèze are spoken of as having pre-existed together in the mind of God. The Jesuit father, when speaking of them, reveals that God conceived them «dans un rapport inextinguible!» (*T*, II, 669). Prouhèze tells the angel that she believes from the bottom of her heart that Rodrigue was created and put in the world for her (*T*, II, 816). The angel seems to substantiate her belief when he asks how Prouhèze could ever exist other than for Rodrigue, since it is through him that she exists (*T*, II, 819).

Claudel tells us that lovers possess the keys to each other's souls. He asserts: «Non, il n'est pas sûr, qu'au-delà de la vie, deux âmes aient été faites pour autre chose que de servir de clef l'une à l'autre» (*T,* I, 1342). In addition, they seem to have some knowledge of each other prior to meeting and are therefore on the lookout for one another. Their encounter is then always accompanied by recognition. Ysé tells Mesa: «Moi, avant que tu ne me connaisses, j'étais là / Quelqu'un qui t'appelait et que tu t'es rappelé» (*T,* I, 1194). She was waiting for him as he was waiting for her. Similarly, Marthe seems to have been waiting for Louis and Musique for the Viceroy. Claudelian lovers are also said to find their necessity in each other. They are necessary because of each other. They complete one another. Rodrigue informs us that Prouhèze needed him to become herself and Ysé tells Mesa she is «le double de toi avec moi, et tu es le double de moi avec toi» (*T,* I, 1110). Finally, Claudel speaks of «cet être complet que prévoyait déjà Platon, somme toute, à sa manière, et dans laquelle un être n'est complet qu'en étant deux en un, qu'en se servant de chacun de l'autre pour être lui-même» (*Mi,* 340).

The recurrence of the theme of fascination or love at first sight in Claudel's work (with all its concomitant subthemes —i.e., predestination, foreknowledge, recognition, and necessity) can cause much perplexity. Some, particularly the Catholic apologists, might find it difficult to reconcile theories of predestination, for instance, with orthodox Catholicism. Others might be tempted to make too much of the influences which were purportedly to have molded Claudel's thinking in this sphere. One could also make the mistake of dismissing the whole theme as unimportant—a mere remnant of romanticism.

We should not forget, however, that Claudel, the man, underwent experiences similar to those he describes in his plays. His encounter with Rosalie L. aboard the Ernest-Simons apparently had all the earmarks of an experience which might be described as love at first sight. He was thunderstruck. And we know of the heightened importance he ascribed to this motif after 1901. (The few and relatively unimportant instances in which it appears in Claudel's literary production prior to 1901 are, I think, indeed attributable to a romantic residue.) I am convinced that Claudel's recourse to the Bible, to Plato and Dante, or to Buddhism for that matter, served only to reinforce ideas which were already his because of what he had undergone.

It is important at this point to understand all the psychological implications of an experience such as this. We learn from Carl Jung that «fascination is a phenomenon of compulsion which lacks conscious ground; that is, it is not a process of the will, but something that emerges from the unconscious and forcibly obtrudes itself on consciousness» (1). This serves to explain the violence of the emotion and also the feeling that divine will or fate is somehow involved. Next we go on to learn that fascination implies a soul projection. (Projection is defined as «an unconscious, automatic process whereby a content that is unconscious to the subject transfers itself to an object, so that it seems to belong to that object» [2].) This phenomenon, we are then told, usually takes place in men who repress their own feminine traits. We need only recall Tête d'Or's super-*machismo* to realize that this was true of Claudel. We also discover that a man such as this will be attracted by «the woman who best corresponds to his own unconscious femininity, a woman, in short, who can unhesitatingly receive the projection of his soul» (3).

One might ask at this point what type of woman serves best as receptacle for Anima projections. Jung answers that he could almost speak of a definite type. «The so-called

---

(1) Carl G. Jung, *Two Essays on Analytical Psychology*, trans. by H. G. and C. F. Baynes (London: Baillière, Tindall and Cox, 1928), p. 91.
(2) Carl G. Jung, *The Archetypes and the Collective Unconscious*, trans. by R. F. C. Hull, 2nd ed., Bollingen Series XX (Princeton: Princeton University Press, 1968), p. 60.
(3) Jung, *Two Essays*, p. 203.

sphinx-like character is indispensible, ambiguity, a sense of being endowed with many possibilities; not an indefiniteness that offers nothing, but an indefiniteness that is full of promises» (4). The lover needs a woman of this type so he can weave his fantasies around her. He needs to find his «own complexity answered by a corresponding manifoldness» (5). Finding a woman such as this is then of course a momentous occasion. The element of recognition will be operative at such an encounter for the very reason that we are dealing with a soul or Anima projection.

Finally, we are told that fascination «is never exercised exclusively by one person on another. It is a phenomenon of reciprocal relation between two people» (6). Each must offer the right disposition.

How does all of this correlate with Claudel's experience? Before turning to his works for an answer, let us first get an outside opinion. I believe that the following observations made by Agnes Meyer are very revealing. We should keep in mind that she knew Claudel intimately and that she had also met Rosalie L.:

> After the life he had led it was the only thing that could have happened (7).

> The passion evidently was all on the other side and she merely a vessel of it (8).

> It was all so maladif [sic] and had to be so. No matter where he had gone, no matter whom he had met, he could not have escaped. The woman in any case was just an accident. He was ripe for a fall —a smash and along came La Rose to be made the vessel of his pent-up passion and lovelines.... What odd things we are, going about in the world weaving

---

(4) Jung, *Contributions*, p. 200.
(5) Ibid., p. 201.
(6) Jung, *Two Essays*, p. 91.
(7) Meyer, «Note-Book», p. 163.
(8) Ibid., p. 178.

— 31 —

the web of our destiny out of our own entrails and
then fastening it upon other people. She too seems
doomed by queer fixations for she has an obvious
appeal for the neurotic type—Both her husbands
having been that kind.... And yet in her way she
enjoyed it all thoroughly (9).

It is fascinating to note how well these observations tie in
with the above.

Now we can turn to Claudel's works for further evidence
of the fact that what we are dealing with here is an Anima
projection. Let us first call to mind the manner in which
Claudel inevitably associates woman with the soul. One
feels, in fact, that the mysterious qualities attributed to woman
by the poet (as discussed above) stem from this identification.
Women are felt to be, and are portrayed as being, capricious,
elusive, mysterious, and laden with possibilities because
Claudel's muse—the woman living within, his Anima—was
all of these things. (Note how these are the very qualities
that Jung says a woman must possess to be a good container
for an Anima projection. When Ysé says: «Il y a une femme
en moi qui ne pourra pas s'empêcher de vous répondre» [T,
I, 1005], one senses the multiplicity present in her.) We
know that Claudel had had very litle contact with women
when he created characters such as Lala and Lechy. And
we also know that he consistently admits to the fact that
most of the characters in his plays represent different aspects
of himself. The women in Claudel's theatre are then varying
portraits of his Anima.

Claudel's heroes and heroines often make reference to this
identification between women and the soul. Mesa says to
Ysé: «Tu es mon coeur, et mon âme, et le défaut de mon
âme» (T, I, 1042). Rodrigue tells us: «Mon âme est vide.
À cause de celle qui n'est pas là» (T, II, 914). Pensée
informs Orian: «C'est de cela que vous manquez et que je

_____
(9) Ibid., p. 184.

fus faite» (*T*, II, 545). And finally, Musique claims a place for herself beneath the Viceroy's heart (*T*, II, 766). In all of these instances not only is the woman associated with the soul, but she is also linked with Eve who, if we remember, was removed from Adam's side, at a point beneath his heart, leaving behind a void which Claudel calls the soul.

Taking this concept into account—the concept that the soul is a void—it might then be said that Claudel's conscious view of what happened to him when he met Ysé is almost an exact mirror image of reality. He was thunderstruck, as are the characters in his plays, at finding someone whom he believed to be capable of filling the void which was his soul—the empty need which was his soul—like a key might fill the lock for which it was made. He speaks in terms of something outside us of which we unfortunately have been deprived. He speaks of nostalgia and of an absence desperately felt. He explains in the following manner: «Le besoin est une espèce d'image négative de la satisfaction qu'il appelle; il est la représentation constante chez le sujet de l'objet qui est destiné à la remplir. Comme ce besoin est constant, ainsi l'énergie qui pousse l'être vivant à chercher hors de lui où et de quoi le contenter, ainsi les qualités dans l'objet extérieur à cet effet disposées, ainsi les signes auxquels cet objet est *reconnu* (car rien de connu, s'il n'est connu d'avance)» (*Opo*, 177).

This is how we might assume Claudel would account for love at first sight and recognition. This is also how one might explain, in Claudelian terms, the fact that in both Lechy and Lala the poet was able to draw portraits of the future Ysé. He says of Ysé: «Elle se dessinait par son vide» (*Mi*, 94).

This theory doesn't stand up under close scrutiny, however. And Claudel's lack of lucidity can easily be explained by the fact that, as stated above, the phenomenon of fascination is basically an unconscious process which derives its very impact from this characteristic. Claudel's whole theory is based on the conviction, arrived at through intellectual means, that

3

the soul is a void. Reference is made to this belief on many occasions. Yet, with even more frequency, the soul is referred to as a woman living within. (See Chapter I.) Since these designations are obviously difficult to reconcile, we ask ourselves which of the two is more authentic for Claudel. When we realize that the first is the product of oriental influence, on the one hand, and of shaky Biblical exegesis, on the other; whereas, the second seems to be the natural product of personal creative experience, we know which designation to opt for. We might also add that if the soul is a void and foreknowledge comes only through an absence felt, how then was Mesa able to say to Ysé: «Et qu'est-ce que j'ai fait, toutes ces années où je t'attendais, que de penser à toi et de m'habituer à toi? Toutes ces heures, toutes ces minutes dans mon lit où je te tenais dans mes bras!» (*T,* I, 1192)? It seems instead that in this passage Mesa's foreknowledge is attributable to something more concrete than a need. We are dealing with a woman whom Claudel has himself identified with the soul («Elle [Ysé] se dessinait par son vide»— vide=âme). She is the woman living within. Claudel often associates her with his muse. We also know that his female characters were created in her image. Lechy and Lala are in her image. And we must conclude that Ysé only conformed to the pattern because Claudel projected that same image on to her. Rather than perfectly filling the void which was his soul, I contend, she was instead the perfect vessel for his Anima projection. She was the void which he filled with his soul. And I feel that it was because Claudel sensed the identification between her and his soul that he devised the theory mentioned above which only appears in the works written after his encounter.

In an interesting article on *Partage de midi* Bernard Howells points to the fact that the definitions Ysé gives of herself are always definitions of Mesa's feelings towards her (10). This observation is supportive of my contention as is

---

(10) Bernard Howells, «The Enigma of *Partage de midi:* A

Agnes Meyer's appraisal of Claudel's love affair, cited above. For further substantiation I might quote a passage from the second version of *La Ville*. It is Lala who is speaking:

> Mais l'alliance et l'hymen qu'un homme conclut avec une femme
> Est insuffisant, et l'amour s'épuise comme l'amitié.
> Comme une note comporte la série sans fin de ses harmoniques, jusqu'aux deux termes de l'ouïe,
> Chaque homme, *pour vivre toute son âme*, appelle de multiples accords [the italics are mine] (*T*, I, 462).

Here we see the love relationship clearly linked with the phenomenon of Anima projection.

I might also add that all of this lends a measure of intelligibility to some of the Claudelian attitudes on women discussed in the first part of this chapter. Once we understand the role played by Claudel's Anima in the love relationship, we can also understand why Claudel found women so enigmatic, why he said they represent something other than what they are, why his heroes are duped and misled by them, why they so often appear veiled, and why the love relationship is seen to increase the hero's self-knowledge while it in no way increases his comprehension of his mate. Claudel says: «La manière justement de se connaître c'est l'amour» (*Mi*, 340). Mesa learns much about himself as a result of his affair with Ysé, yet she remains a puzzle to him.

We already know that this lack of understanding and comprehension on the part of the male results from the fact that the soul is indeed mysterious. What we now discover is that it is also the natural outgrowth of a projection. When a projection is made, the vessel of the projection is never

---

Study in Ambiguity», in *Claudel: A Reappraisal*, p. 28. In this article Howells speaks of the «projection on to Ysé of a suppressed pattern of sexual feelings in Claudel». This viewpoint is interesting but it doesn't fully explain the phenomenon of fascination, particularly the connection between Ysé and the soul.

really known or comprehended by her lover. Her behavior will then seen strange, unmotivated, and erratic. We learn from Jung that very few women are able, in the long run, to correspond consistently with the soul-image projected on them and as a result, this type of love relation is very unstable.

Before continuing with an investigation of other aspects of the love relationship, I would like to briefly discuss Claudel's views on the institution of marriage. I choose to do this now for a very simple reason—it is a theme which is as problematic as the theme of love at first sight, and this for the same reasons. Again, some who might find it necessary to do so, would not be able to reconcile Claudelian thought with traditional orthodoxy.

The reason is always the same for any departure on Claudel's part from the straight and narrow path of orthodoxy. He was, as we all are, a product of the experiences he had had in life, and it is common knowledge that Claudel's marriage was not a love match. It is said that he told his fiancée prior to their union: «Mademoiselle, je vous promettrai une fidélité que je vous garderai sur terre avec la loyauté que vous devez attendre de moi, mais pour votre ciel, ne comptez pas sur moi. Mon ciel appartient à une autre âme de façon irrévocable» (11). In 1906 he wrote to Suarès: «Ne croyez pas que mon mariage me fasse oublier mes amis; ce n'est qu'un moyen de m'assurer contre certains dangers» (12). This being the case, one is not surprised to find that most of his comments on marriage are negative.

Early in his *Journal* Claudel states: «L'amour dans le mariage vit tout entier sur ce que les coureurs appellent le 'second wind'» (*J, I, 213*). Later he compares the conjugal relationship to a monastic cell which keeps us locked up, imprisoned. The pope in *Le Père humilié* tells us that this union is not pleasure—it is the sacrifice of pleasure. Pensée

---

(11) *L'Express,* Feb. 12-18, 1968, p. 29.
(12) André Suarès and Paul Claudel, *Correspondance 1904-1938* (Paris: Gallimard, 1951), p. 63.

associates it with death when she exclaims: «La myrrhe nuptiale! la funèbre myrrhe!» (*T, II, 568*). Claudel goes even further when he says this relationship is «le fondement de l'ordre social, le sacrifice mutuel et permanent sur lequel il repose, à l'imitation de celui du Calvaire et de la Messe» (*Opr, 530*). Pélage informs us that it is not love which makes a marriage but instead the act of two people consenting to one another. Orian adds that his passion is incompatible with this institution. We also learn that Claudel calls Ysé's union with De Ciz an obstacle barring «le chemin de Dieu» (*T, I, 1339*). For woman the marriage day is termed the day of her humiliation and the continuing relationship is referred to as conjugal servitude. In Claudel's theatre the number of unhappy marriages (unions in which only one of the partners is in love with the other) is staggering. We have: Baube and Lidine, Mara and Jacques, to some extent Marthe and Louis, Sygne and Turelure, Sichel and Louis, Pensée and Orso, Ysé and De Ciz, Prouhèze and Pélage, Prouhèze and Camille, Isabel and Ramire, and Hélène and Ménélas.

There are, however, some instances in his prose works and in his poetry when Claudel exalts this institution. (He goes so far as to call it the great sacrament, the sacrament par excellence.) And there are also one or two examples of happy marriages in his theatre. We could cite Musique and the Viceroy, the father and mother in *Annonce faite à Marie* (although he does leave her) and finally, one suspects that Don Diègue and Dona Austrégésile will have a happy union, considering the love and fidelity demonstrated by both. These examples, however, are few and far between and one is left to conclude that by and large Claudel's view of marriage was highly negative.

I would now like to continue my study of the love relationship as seen in Claudel's works by examining the nature of the sexual act. Claudel tells us that physical love is in effect the mystery of mysteries, allied to the most profound religious mysteries: generation, creation, and the communion of two souls. He explains that for Catholics man is considered to be naturally destined to happiness and none of the efforts he makes to reach this goal is thought of as being evil in and of itself. Sensual or sexual pleasure is not only permitted, «elle est voulue par l'Évangile, parce que l'Évangile, c'est la nature, et que la nature, c'est la jouissance, et cela aujourd'hui, pas demain, ... SUR CETTE TERRE D'ADAM ET D'ÈVE!» (*J*, I, 221). We learn that the love two people give to one another is so great a thing in God's eyes that He has made of it a sacrament. Woman was created to be desirable; therefore, the desire she arouses is of itself good and holy.

The union of man and woman—the actual sexual spasm—is called a moment which is all eternity, a detonation in which all time is abolished. In this glorious instant the lovers are said to cross over into Eden. They reachieve a primitive integrality.

This union, we learn, is intimately connected with creation. When in Ysé's embrace, Mesa tells us he feels within him «le profond dérangement / De la création, comme la Terre / Lorsque l'écume aux lèvres elle produisait la chose aride, et que dans un rétrécissement effroyable / Elle faisait sortir sa substance et le repli des monts comme de la pâte!» (*T,* I, 1027). As we can see, however, this creative experience is not associated with reproduction, for its effects are operative within the male. Mesa affirms this when he states: «Il ne s'agit pas d'un enfant! c'est lui pour naître, on ne sait comment, / Qui profite de ce moment que nous trouvons de l'éternité» (*T,* I, 996). What we are in fact dealing with here is the creativity connected with spiritual rebirth. The Princess explains: «La Femme qui vous aime voudrait vous être mère!» (*T,* I, 64). Marthe reaffirms this. She would like to give new spiritual life to her husband. In fact, Claudel tells us that Louis penetrated her because there was no other way for him to pass over into that other realm. Prouhèze also makes claims similar to those of Marthe: «Il n'y a rien dans son corps et âme que je ne sois capable de

tenir avec moi pour toujours dans le sommeil de la douleur /
Comme Adam, quand il dormit, la première femme» (*T*, II,
779). She also would like to give life to her lover. Just
as Adam in a deep sleep conceived Eve, now it is Eve's turn
to give birth to Adam thereby repairing the damage inflicted
when she led him astray.

What must man do to cooperate in this operation? We
discover he must surrender himself completely to his mate.
He must give her his all—his life. «C'est vrai», says Marthe,
«ce n'est pas moi qui t'ai donné la vie. / Mais je suis ici
pour te la redemander» (*T*, I, 670). Her exigency resembles
God's for she is His instrument. Man must then die to
himself and to the world before he can be reborn. And in
keeping with this the sex act involves the sort of death
implicit in total surrender and total love. Ysé tells us: «Il
faut se laisser faire, / Il faut mourir / Entre les bras de celui
qui l'aime» (*T*, I, 996). In other words, one must love
totally. Death, we learn, comes of love. («Plus on aime,
plus on a de mort» [13].) On a different level, physical union
is also likened to re-entrance in the womb—another death:
«J'étais enfoncé en toi jusqu'aux narines ainsi que dans un
trou profond» (*T*, I, 1044). What then can be achieved in
the love act is the giving of oneself which necessarily preludes
eternal life. (And we have seen how the orgasm is called
a moment which is all eternity.) Violaine states: «Il suffit
d'un moment pour mourir, et la mort même l'un dans l'autre /
Ne nous anéantira pas plus que l'amour» (*T*, II, 54). So
in effect what woman gives is also what she requires: a
death which leads to life—the death of re-entrance into the
womb and also the death of complete renunciation, complete
love.

At this point one might well ask if woman also participates in this new birth which she imparts to her mate. The
following passage from the second version of *La Jeune Fille*

_____

(13) Suarès, *Correspondance*, p. 49.

Violaine, in which Pierre is speaking to Violaine, seems to furnish a reply: «L'amour que vous allez connaître est semblable à l'humiliation de la mort, à la résolution de la dernière heure, / Et *un homme nouveau naît* de ce consentement réciproque, du double et funèbre aveu [italics are mine]» (*T,* I, 579). We see here that woman also must give of herself completely, she must love completely. She too must die to have new life. We also discover that the lovers are reborn as one flesh. A new *man* comes to life —a new Adam, with the feminine principle restored. The primitive integrality reappears. Woman is reborn with her lover, within her lover.

It is perhaps now time to bring up a factor which has been missing in our discussion thus far but which is intimately connected with much that was dealt with above. This factor is sin—the corrupting element introduced in the Garden of Eden which is now so closely associated with the love relationship that woman herself is identified with the tree of the knowledge of good and of evil and with its fruit. Pierre cries to Violaine: «O jeune arbre de la science du Bien et du Mal, voici que je commence à me séparer parce que j'ai porté la main sur vous. / Et déjà mon âme et mon corps se divisent» (*T,* II, 16). Not only are the wages of sin death, but we also discover that sin is a kind of death in and of itself. Claudel speaks of «cette seconde mort de tous les jours» (*T,* II, 272) which is mortal sin. This being the case we can understand why what woman offers is not always the death which ushers us into eternal life but may well be the death attached to sin which leaves one «aux portes du Néant».

Sin, we learn, almost completely vitiates the relationship between the sexes. That is why darkness, a funereal shame, and penitential bitterness are now so often associated with the union of man and woman. True love was only possible in the Garden of Eden. Sin prevents man from attributing a proper goal to the love relationship. Through sin woman herself becomes man's goal and thus an obstacle to his rebirth rather than the instrument of his rebirth. «C'est toi qui m'ouvres le paradis et c'est toi qui m'empêches d'y rester. Comment serais-je avec tout quand tu me refuses d'être autre part qu'avec toi? / Chaque pulsation de ton coeur avec moi me rend le supplice, cette impuissance à échapper au paradis dont tu fais que je suis exclu» (*T*, II, 781). Herein lies the danger often alluded to of loving too much.

Even more devastating, however, is the fact that sin obstructs our desire to give completely of ourselves, which we know to be the prime requisite for complete union. Without this death—the death of total surrender—there can be no life. Claudel says: «À aucun moment l'homme qui enfreint la Loi n'est capable de se donner complètement» (*T*, I, 1338). We see, for instance, how Mesa was unable to surrender completely to Ysé. He knew that this was the requirement («Il faudrait se donner à elle tout entier!» [*T*, I, 999]), but he was unable to comply. As a result their love failed. Ysé explains «Je sentais qu'il était captif, / Mais que je ne le possédais pas, et quelque chose en lui d'étranger / Impossible. / Qu'a-t-il donc à me reprocher? parce qu'il ne s'est pas donné, et moi, je me suis retirée» (*T*, I, 1040-41). Orian also has similar problems. He says: «Ce qu'elle demande, je ne peux le lui donner» (*T*, II, 534). Yet he protests his love, but the Pope in his lucidity tells him: «Ce n'est pas aimer quelqu'un que de ne pas lui donner ce qu'on a en soi de meilleur» (*T*, II, 533). There is something within which says no—a denial which is not on the physical plane but rather on a spiritual level and it impedes total union.

Yet despite this failure to give of themselves completely, the lovers still feel a desperate need for one another and often try to achieve their goal by strictly physical means. We soon learn, however, that this goal cannot be achieved by these means. «Les moyens charnels ne suffisent pas à agencer ces deux êtres l'un à l'autre. La chair ne leur fournit que la constatation désespérée de leur impuissance l'un par rapport à l'autre» (*T*, I, 1345). We also go on to discover that desire for the flesh is in no way diminished by this awareness and that with each renewed attempt at union this awareness is heightened. Ysé says: «Mais avec lui c'était le désespoir et le désir» (*T*, I, 1040). Inevitably, however, the lovers come to think that it is the flesh which is the impediment to union. (It is easier to claim this than to admit that one has held back.) Ysé speaks of «la rage, et la tendresse, et de te détruire et de n'être plus gêné / Détestablement par ces vêtements de chair» (*T*, I, 1026). In *L'Homme et son désir* Claudel describes the dance of passion as follows: «Un mouvement de va-et-vient de plus en plus ardent et désespéré, comme l'animal qui rencontre la paroi et revient sans cesse à la même place» (*T*, II, 644). This wall is undoubtedly intended to symbolize the flesh.

All of this obviously reflects Claudel's own personal experiences. And that being the case, we can understand why his view of sexual union while positive in some respects (as indicated above) is also so often negative. He has gone so far as to say that possession actually destroys that which is sublime in passion. He explains: «L'amour humain n'a de beauté que quand il n'est pas accompagné par la satisfaction ... Quant aux voluptés de l'amour satisfait, aucun écrivain ne les a jamais dépeintes, car elles n'existent pas» (14). Elsewhere he remarks: «Non, la satisfaction sexuelle n'est pas celle de la passion et de l'amour, elle en est un rétrécissement parfois caricatural, une déformation le plus souvent et toujours une transformation. Il ne s'agit pas là de finesses platoniciennes» (15). Similar statements run all the way through Claudel's works. Orian remarks: «Ce qu'on appelle l'amour, / C'est toujours le même calembour final, la même coupe tout de suite vidée, l'affaire de quelques nuits d'hôtel, et de nouveau / La foule, la bagarre ahurissante» (*T*, II, 545).

(14) Jacques Rivière and Paul Claudel, *Correspondance 1907-1914* (Paris: Plon-Nourrit et Cie, 1926), p. 262.
(15) Paul Claudel and André Gide, *Correspondance 1899-1926* (Paris: Gallimard, 1949), p. 101.

Mesa adds: «Tout amour n'est qu'une comédie / Entre l'homme et la femme; les questions ne sont pas posées» (*T*, I, 996). Physical love obviously becomes empty and meaningless—a bitter disappointment—when it isn't accompanied by a spiritual giving.

Now we may ask ourselves: Why exactly was Claudel (and therefore his heroes) unable to give of himself completely in a love relationship? How precisely does sin enter into the picture? We sense that there are many possible answers to these questions. The most obvious centers around two facts: that his affair with R. L. was illicit and that he went into marriage without love. It is understandable that a highly religious man not give himself over completely in an adulterous affair, even though he may have wanted to. «Il y a le désir qui veut, mais il y a quelque chose en nous de plus ancien que le désir, qui ne veut pas» (*T*, II, 1475). In keeping with this he also says: «La vue même de l'enfer sous mes pas ne m'aurait pas séparé de cette ennemie! Il a fallu que Dieu intervînt par un coup de force; il est vrai que j'avais prié pour cela» (16). The feeling of interdiction was over-whelming. «Ce paradis que Dieu ne m'a pas ouvert et que tes bras pour moi ont refait un court moment, ah! femme, tu ne me le donnes que pour me communiquer que j'en suis exclu. / Chacun de tes baisers me donne un paradis dont je sais qu'il m'est interdit» (*T*, II, 781). It is also under-standable that he not give himself completely in a luke-warm marriage. It was Claudel's personal tragedy that the love experience came to him outside of wedlock.

All of this is well and good but, as we suspected, it does not constitute a full explanation. We must look further to explain, for example, why Orian, who was not involved in an adulterous affair, was unable to surrender himself or why the love relationships in *Tête d'Or* or *La Ville*, imagined by Claudel prior to 1901, are also unsuccessful. If we recall,

---

(16) Suarès, *Correspondance*, p. 48-49.

however, some of the feminine characteristics outlined in the first part of this chapter, we will find ample reason for this and also another explanation for Claudel's attitudes. It is abundantly clear that Claudel, particularly in his early years, found woman to be an inadequate, an unworthy object for his love. To evidence this we need only bring to mind Henri in *Fragment d'un drame* who vows never to leave Marie and then feels a sudden repulsion, or Tête d'Or who heaps vituperation on women. There are also many instances in which women are compared to animals (Ysé is «la sale bête» and Marie is «la chienne», for instance) and/or are treated like animals—flung over a man's shoulder, for example. Claudel feels that, in reality, woman is something other than what she represents (the soul, the Church, Mary, and Sophia). When he speaks of «toutes ces choses que nous aimons tant et qui dans le fond nous dégoûtent» (*Opo*, 500), we know women fit into this category.

This attitude is partially explainable by the defective comprehension of women possessed by the male. He senses that she contains a promise for him but he is unable to discern what that promise is, often making the mistake of thinking that it is contained in her body alone. The following dialogue between Rodrigue and Camille illustrates this point:

> DON RODRIGUE.—Mais d'abord j'attendais d'elle cette chose qu'elle seule peut me donner.
> DON CAMILLE.—Quelle chose?
> DON RODRIGUE.—Comment la connaîtrai-je autrement qu'en la recevant?
> DON CAMILLE.—Cette chose mystérieuse, pourquoi ne pas dire qu'elle ne fait qu'un avec son corps?
> DON RODRIGUE.—Il est vrai. Comment comprendre? (*T*, II, 772).

The lover misunderstands woman's mission. He misunderstands what she requires of him and also misunderstands what she has to offer. Ysé says to Mesa: «Tu ne me demandais que mon corps et moi c'est bien autre chose que je te demandais» (*T*, I, 1138). Prouhèze feels that her body was denied to

Rodrigue because he would have loved it too much. We might add that he also would have hated it eventually. The Claudelian lover does not want to give his soul because he feels woman is unworthy to receive it. Yet, despite this, he loves and desires her flesh because of his own physical needs. He even hopes to achieve real union with woman through her body. So he attaches himself to it only to experience bitter disappointment. Claudel speaks of «le besoin supérieur à son sujet, le désir plus nécessaire que la vie, / [qui] Se retourne, inhabile à recevoir comme il est impuissant à donner, / Contre ce misérable coeur qu'il n'arrive pas à déraciner!» (*Opo*, 625).

There are still other reasons though for Claudel's failure. The above doesn't explain, for instance, why Claudel was unable to give himself completely over to God, the perfect object for our love. Ysé chides Mesa: «On fait semblant de tout donner, alors qu'au fond, ah pour être décidé, on est bien décidé à tout garder pour soi. C'est comme ça que jadis on s'est offert au bon Dieu, mon petit Mesa» (*T*, I, 1137). There is undoubtedly a great deal of self-centeredness involved here. We know Mesa is «un vilain petit bougre de sacré d'égoiste» (*T*, I, 1138). But the problem goes deeper than mere egoism. There seems to exist in Claudel a deep-rooted fear of the death implicit in surrender, whether it be surrender to God or to woman. This is a fear which Ysé claims is common to all men: «O comme les hommes sont durs et fermés, et comme ils ont donc peur de souffrir et de mourir! / Mais la femelle Femme, mère de l'homme / Ne s'étonne point, familière aux mains taciturnes qui tirent» (*T*, I, 1058). Ysé speaks of the death required in love when she remarks: «Il ne faut pas comprendre, mon pauvre monsieur! / Il faut perdre connaissance». We then see Claudel project his own feeling on to her when he has her add: «Moi, je suis trop méchante, je ne puis pas» (*T*, I, 995-96). Ysé is also expressing his sentiments when she states: «Je ne veux point me donner tout entière / Et je ne veux pas mourir, mais je suis jeune / Et la mort n'est pas belle» (*T*,

I, 1005). Even Musique, who is so giving by nature and to whose love there are no obstacles, echoes these feelings. When the Viceroy asks her: «Quel est ce visage effrayé que je vois dans la lumière de la lune?», she answers: «C'est mon âme qui essaye de se défendre et qui fuit en poussant des cris entrecoupés» (*T*, II, 764). Orian also expresses similar reticence. The key to this fear is found, I believe, in the following passage: «Je ne suis pas un ascète hindou, je ne suis pas prêt à me liquéfier comme une poupée de sel, comme disent les mystiques hindous, dans une mer de délices, une mer de joies. Ce n'est pas du tout mon sentiment. Je ne perds jamais le sentiment de ma personnalité» (*Mi*, 160). Egoism? Yes, but also a dread of losing one's identity, of being swallowed by something larger than oneself.

Still other misgivings exist, however. But before we can understand them, we must first explore another aspect of Claudel's thinking. Claudel tells us that when he was still very young he came to the realization that he was one of those men whose vocation it would be to gather all that presented itself before them «et d'en faire un objet d'une espèce de conquête» (*Mi*, 355). Man, he explains, was not made to be contained in creation but rather to vanquish it, dominate it, to reunite its parts, to wrench from it what meaning it may contain. This aggressive posture, with its implied violence, is one of the basic components of Claudel's make-up. Tête d'Or proclaims: «En cela que quelque chose ne m'est pas soumis je ne suis pas libre ... Que rien ne soit hors de moi! ... Que je me saisisse du monde infini, il n'est pas trop peu petit pour moi?» (*T*, I, 96).

It was of prime importance to Claudel that he not be numbered among the vanquished. Too often had he seen the horror of artists crushed by life—Verlaine, Villiers de l'Isle-Adam, and, of course, his own sister—to permit similar defeat in his own case. He would be a victor in life, he would succeed. With his intellect he would dominate reality. (Knowledge for him was a triumph over the object, a conquest which permitted one to comprehend the manner in which it was made and which permitted one to recreate it within oneself.) He thrived on any opposition encountered. Opposition and resistance, we learn, result in heightened consciousness. This is one of the reasons why open hostility is said to be beneficial. Claudel remarks: «On ne connaît jamais bien une chose que quand cette chose vous fait souffrir» (*Mi*, 129). After wrestling with Mesa, Amalric exclaims: «C'est drôle comme on se comprend quand on se bat avec quelqu'un» (*T*, I, 1131). Warfare is also lauded: «C'est elle qui fait sortir de nous du nouveau et de l'inouï» (*Opr*, 722). The following is one of Claudel's most severe criticisms of the Chinese: «Il n'a ni la joie de se battre, la plus grande que puisse éprouver chez nous un homme normal et sain, ni celle de donner enfin tout son plein d'énergie, ni le désir de vaincre» (*Opr*, 1073).

The instincts of domination were so strong in Claudel that we see many of his characters almost willingly forsake everything to pursue a vocation involving conquests of some kind (including conquest of the hereafter). The so-called sacrifices of so many Claudelian heroes and heroines should, I believe, be re-examined in this light. We sense, for instance, that secretly both Prouhèze and Rodrigue more than welcome the sacrifice required of them. Prouhèze exclaims: (Ah! si j'étais un homme, ce n'est pas une femme qui me ferait renoncer à l'Afrique! Voilà une chose qui résiste! Il y en a pour toute la vie!» (*T*, II, 742). As Pélage explains, «elle a trouvé son destin et son destin l'a trouvée; qui l'a une fois connue ne s'en sépare pas aisément» (*T*, II, 754). And Camille is not far from wrong when he says to Rodrigue: «Car il a tout de même cette Amérique au fond de vous, plus ancienne que ce visage de femme qui vous travaille et à quoi ce serait tellement dommage de renoncer. Comme je vous comprends!» (*T*, II, 770).

These aggressive instincts are also carried over into the love relationship. Claudel also wanted to dominate in this sphere. He tells us that there is no combination without subordination and it is clear that Claudel would not be the subordinate member of any couple. The interaction between the sexes is likened to combat between enemy forces. Ysé, for instance, is called a warrior and a conqueror.

It is written, however, that woman should be subservient to man. As Tête d'Or tells us, she was made to stay at home and to submit to her husband. So in order to bring this to pass man must vanquish and subdue her. Avare remarks that his father took his mother by force and kept her through terror. Woman is like a city besieged whose protective walls must be demolished. Claudel speaks of «le gémissement de l'amant qui obtient le corps bestial entre ses bras de la bien-aimée après le long combat» (*Opo, 280*). When Lala submits to Coeuvre, he puts his foot on her prostrate body in a gesture of triumph.

The relationship between man and woman is also compared to the ties between hunter and hunted. Woman is man's prey. Laeta says: «Car à quoi sert d'être une femme sinon pour être cueillie? / Et cette rose sinon pour être dévorée? Et d'être jamais née / Sinon pour être à un autre et la proie d'un puissant lion?» (*Opo, 340*). In *Fragment d'un drame* Henri tells us that when he first saw Marie he pounced on her and took her, like a wolf carrying off his prey. *Tête d'Or* opens with a similar image—Simon Agnel with a woman's body flung over his shoulder. Ysé is called the supreme prey and, vanquished, she is compared to «un gibier qui plie et que l'on tient par la nuque!» (*T, I, 1023*).

All of this, however, has other implications of which Claudel is only too painfully aware. Woman may be man's prey, but man is the victim of his need for her and herein lies much of her power. Man's nature presupposes woman and just as the lion hungers after the lamb, man yearns for woman. And we know that Claudel's flesh was particularly demanding. He tells us that it took him all the spiritual strength he could muster to combat the longings of his body. These earthly desires are so overwhelming that Brindosier says: «Qui reprocherait à un dieu dans sa joie de prendre la forme d'une bête, s'il ne peut s'en empêcher, / Une fois qu'il a pris l'odeur de la terre, plus forte que celle d'un lion ou de troupeaux fumants» (*T*, II, 312). This being the case, we can understand comments such as the following taken from Claudel's *Journal:* «Ces belles femmes q[ui] sont un danger public et qu'on devrait mettre en prison!» (*J*, II, 353). Woman is a danger, almost a public menace because she stirs in man longings which he has difficulty controlling. She is also called «la grande humiliatrice» for despite all his brutality, when a man falls in love he comes under her power —a power which paralyzes him. In Claudel's mind to love is to assume a position of weakness vis-à-vis the loved one. He remarks: «Hélas! celui qui aime se place en état d'infériorité» (*J*, I, 304).

Here then is the final reason for Claudel's failure in love. He would not allow himself to be vanquished by the enemy despite, or perhaps because of her enormous power. The role of conquering hero was not harmonious with a love that required surrender. (We sense that he also resented the violence with which this love was thrust upon him. He felt as though he had fallen into a trap from which it was impossible to escape. His freedom had been usurped.) Claudel describes the humiliation of the love experience in *Festin de la Sagesse* where we are presented with the following tableau: A woman with a rope at the end of which is tied a blindfolded man. This man, with an enormous head of hair like Samson, has a lion skin draped on his back. The woman is pulling the man along with all her might. The man resists but the woman drags him on inexorably. Here man has become woman's prey. The roles have been reversed because he has allowed himself to love. Ysé says that there is nothing weaker than a man in a woman's arms. He is like something which has fallen to earth and can fall no farther.

For these reasons the love a man bears a woman is often referred to as a sickness or disease which bring him suffering and saps his energy. Rodrigue compares Prouhèze's presence within him to the plague or leprosy, both devouring maladies.

4

We know that Pierre contracted this latter dread disease after attempting to force himself on Violaine. To describe further the devastating effects of love Claudel has recourse to an old romantic theme. Love is a mortal wound inflicted by woman with her beauty. Pierre and Jacques speak of it as do Cébès and Rodrigue. Orian too has been wounded.

Interestingly enough, the women in Claudel's theatre also speak of having received a similar wound. But somehow, just as weakness and submissiveness are considered to be desirable attributes in woman—attributes which characterize a natural condition to which she herself aspires (Ysé pleads: «Empêche / Que je redevienne cette ancienne Ysé, la guerrière, Ysé, Ysé la folle!» [*T*, I, 1357])—this wounding of woman is thought of as being the natural, inevitable consequence of her contact with man. It is in the image of the wounding wrought through sexual penetration. When Violaine avers «le mâle est prêtre, mais il n'est pas défendu à la femme d'être victime» (*T*, II, 74), we sense that for Claudel this is in the natural order.

It is, however, still surprising to note the degree to which women are victimized in Claudel's plays. In *L'Échange,* for instance, Louis tells Marthe that he actually enjoys hurting her. Similarly, in *L'Otage* Georges de Coûfontaine admits to Sygne: «Il faut que je vous fasse de la peine! c'est ma façon de vous aimer» (*T*, II, 222). We also know of Turelure's treatment of her. With respect to Sichel, we learn that Turelure put a stop to her musical career out of sheer cruelty. Sichel, who was a pianist of world renown, claims that his only motive in taking up with her was to prevent her from playing the piano. In *Partage de midi* Amalric confesses that he finds pleasure in saying cruel things to Ysé and in *Soulier de satin* Camille is known to torture and whip Prouhèze. We even see him twist her arm and bite her. Then of course we also have the brutal and inhuman sacrifices imposed upon women. The Princess in *Tête d'Or* is nailed to a tree. Sygne is required to marry a man she detests, a man who has the blood of her parents on his hands. She then is accused of violating the sacrament of marriage by not loving him.

We are already familiar with many of the reasons for this treatment. We have seen that the sensual powers women wield are deeply resented. We know of the wound they inflict. Prouhèze says she is a sword in Rodrigue's heart. We are also aware of the fact that women seem capricious and deceptive to men. And of course they can be unfaithful. We know of the suffering endured because of Ysé's betrayal. Then there is the frustration and disappointment of physical love which is accompanied by the feeling that woman promises more than she can deliver. In addition, we can cite the tyranny suffered by Claudel at the hands of his sister Camille in their youth.

On another level, however, there are more archaic grievances. When speaking of Eve, Claudel mentions «cette énorme déchirure à son flanc que pour apparaître elle lui a faite!» (*Oc,* XXIII, 32). Here again we see man being wounded by woman. Woman of course also led man astray and is accused of continuing to do so today. It was then because of woman that Christ had to suffer and die. She is responsible for the nails, the whip, the crown of thorns, and the grave.

On yet another level, we discover that the spiritual powers women possess are also feared and resented. Louis admits to Marthe: «Tu es constante et unie, ... Tu es comme une lampe allumée, et où tu es, il fait clair. / C'est pourquoi il arrive que j'ai peur et je voudrais me cacher de toi» (*T,* I, 686-87). Because of her creative capabilities woman inspires awe and trepidation. Tête d'Or says: «Mais nous pouvons ne nous pas cacher / Des yeux de la femme qui enfante» (*T,* I, 157). And Marthe further elucidates the situation when she explains: «C'est vrai, ce n'est pas moi qui t'ai donné la vie, / Mais je suis ici pour te la redemander. Et de là vient à l'homme devant la femme / Ce trouble, tel que la conscience, comme dans la présence du créancier» (*T,* I, 670). As we know, man fears this death. In *Mémoires improvisés* Claudel describes what happens when man comes up against the spiritual power of woman. «Et alors c'est dans *Tête d'Or* que de cette force aveugle, sauvage, cette force instinctive si fréquente chez tous les jeunes gens, trouve plus fort qu'elle en presence de la Princesse; qu'elle est obligée de s'y soumettre, en grinçant des dents plus ou moins» (*Mi*, 63).

All of these factors, coupled with Claudel's own aggressive disposition, serve to explain why woman is so cruelly dealt with in Claudel's theatre. And all of these factors also account for why, with the exception of the poetic idyll of Musique and the Viceroy, there is no example in Claudel's theatre of a love relationship ideally lived, with full surrender. As J. Petit points out: «Claudel peint des amours impossibles, parce que ses personnages ne sauraient vivre ce sentiment» (17). In support of this claim we might cite, as he does, the instances in which the impediments to love are self-imposed or in which love is sacrificed with a strange willingness, a hidden pleasure. Such is the case with Violaine, Sygne, and Prouhèze who actually expresses approval over the fact that her letter did not reach Rodrigue. She states: «Peut-être il vaut mieux qu'il [son appel] ne t'ait pas atteint. / Je n'aurais été qu'une femme bientôt mourante sur ton coeur et non pas cette étoile éternelle dont tu as soif» (*T*, II, 857). Others put up a very feeble struggle or no struggle at all to preserve their love—so it is with Marthe, Louis Turelure, and Orso. Even Rodrigue does not do all that it is in his power to do to possess Prouhèze and as a result Camille asks him: «Mais est-ce que vous l'aimiez? il ne tenait qu'à vous de la prendre» (*T*, II, 770). Love is not impossible in Claudel's universe because of outer obstacles but because of conflicting desires and ambitions and because of the inner fear and reluctance described above.

---

(17) Jacques Petit, *Claudel et l'usurpateur* (Paris: Desclée de Brouwer, 1971), p. 93.

Now that we have examined the failures of Claudel's lovers, let us explore their victories. What did their imperfect and incomplete love yield? What did they achieve through their love? What did they bring to one another? Claudel tells us: «Pour arracher l'homme à lui-même, jusqu'aux racines, pour lui donner le goût de l'Autre, cet avare, ce dur, cet égoiste, pour lui faire préférer monstreusement cet Autre à lui-même, jusqu'à la perdition du corps et de l'âme, il n'y a qu'un instrument approprié, la femme» (T, I, 1341). This is woman's role. She teaches man to prefer something and someone to himself. She vanquishes and melts his hard heart. Claudel feels she was engineered by God to draw man out of himself, to prove to him his nothingness through her own. She teaches him dependance and need. She humbles him and strips him of pride by acquainting him with sin and darkness. Coeuvre says to Lala: «Je sors de tes mains dépouillé» (T, I, 461). She breaks him with the wound she inflicts thereby opening a passage through which God might penetrate, for the soul must be pierced to be made fertile. As Violaine knows, the perfection of our being is to be rent, to be open at last. «A quoi sert le meilleur parfum dans un vase qui est fermé?» (T, II, 89).

Woman forces upon man what he is unable to achieve on his own. Mesa laments: «Déjà elle m'avait détruit le monde et rien pour moi / N'existait qui ne fût pas elle et maintenant elle me détruit moi-même / Et voici qu'elle me fait le chemin plus court» (T, I, 1051-52). Then finally, as though this was not enough, she betrays him, so that the sacrifice imposed might be complete. In this way she again creates a void within him, she leaves him empty. Claudel says that sacrifice always results in a void being created, a void which is a kind of provocation to the divine, a void which represents the elimination «d'un avoir certain au profit d'un crédit éventuel» (Oc, XXIV, 17).

Woman's greatest gift to man is then the suffering she inflicts. It is only this suffering which is capable of evangelizing and converting man's flesh. Through suffering man gains the ability to learn and correct himself. Woman is called «une auberge de peine où il a fallu que nous payions!» (*T,* I, 38). She is also likened to a cross, the cross of suffering on which man's body and soul are quartered. In all of this she is God's instrument. She is also serving Him when she incites that thirst which she cannot quench and when she awakens that desire which she cannot fulfill. She is «la promesse qui ne peut être tenue» (*T,* I, 490) and as such she leads man beyond herself to God for «tant plus nous embrassons d'effets, et tant plus la Cause nous devient indispensable» (*Oc,* XXIII, 303).

It is when the danger arises of too great a love existing between her and her partner that she withdraws, sacrificing their love, betraying him and thereby forcing upon him the renunciation which leads to life. Knowing that union in the here and now will only bring disappointment, through this sacrifice (which Claudel calls «le mariage du non») she attempts to place herself in a higher realm into which she will not only lead and guide but also attract her lover, a realm where their love will be consummated in a greater love. In keeping with this Jacques says to Violaine: «C'est pourquoi il était meilleur, ô Violaine, que je ne vous épouse pas, vous l'avez compris, / Car je vous aimais trop, et afin que cet amour ne soit point trompé, c'est pour cela que vous m'avez trompé. / Passant outre, vous me montrez le chemin, ô tête ensanglantée!» (*T,* I, 654).

This is the so-called Beatrician theme, a theme which does not pertain only to women, however. The role it implies is also fulfilled by certain males in Claudel's theatre. In *Le Père humilié,* for instance, we see how Orian brings salvation to Pensée through the sacrifice of his own life. We also see how the lack of insight and spirituality usually typical of the male in Claudel's universe is here operative in the female. The poet explains: «Le drame consiste dans le malentendu de cette obscurcie qui croit n'avoir besoin que d'un amour humain, tandis que c'est le *salut* qu'en réalité elle demande» (*T,* II, 1418). In keeping with this Orian tells Pensée: «Qu'est-ce que vous aimez, en moi, sinon ce but pour lequel j'ai été fait? sinon ce terme que j'ai été fait pour atteindre et qui m'explique» (*T*, II, 549). Even the role of guide is attributed to the male in this play. Orian beseeches Orso: «Sois à cette âme obscure le guide que je ne puis pas être» (*T*, II, 534). The same is also true elsewhere. Just as in *Le Soulier de satin* Rodrigue «a demandé Dieu à une femme et elle était capable de le lui donner, car il n'y a rien au ciel et sur la terre que l'amour ne soit capable de donner» (*T*, II, 780), in *Partage de midi* Ysé makes the same request of Mesa—he too is required to give what woman gives.

We see then that for Claudel the love relationship is fraught with suffering and pain. It leads to life but only by way of the cross. The lovers are required to sacrifice their lives and their love. At first, they do so in order to achieve a more perfect union with their mates in the hereafter. What passion refuses them in this world they propose to attain in the next through sacrifice. Orian confesses as much when he states: «Si je meurs, Pensée, c'est que sans doute il n'y avait aucun autre moyen pour moi de pénétrer jusqu'à vous!» (*T*, II, 547). This imperfect renunciation, however, does not suffice, for love's true goal is God and we are only instruments used to bring one another to Him. Complete union, as Camille knows, can only be achieved in Him. That is why he says to Prouhèze: «Vous ne serez vraiment à Rodrigue que le jour où cessant d'être à lui vous ne serez qu'à Dieu» (*T*, II, 1087).

Chapter III

THE PARABLE

In his *Journal* Claudel affirms that God is everywhere. He is in all natural phenomena. He is in all human acts. There is nothing—no act, whether good or bad—in which He is not interested, which does not concern Him, which is not related to Him. Claudel then goes on to add: «Tout est parabole, tout signifie l'infinie complexité des rapports des créatures avec leur Créateur. ... Il n'y a rien sur la terre qui ne soit comme la traduction concrète ou déformée du sens qui est dans le ciel» (*J*, I, 587). This is an idea which permeates all of Claudel's works. Nature for him is a symbol and events or history a parable. «Rien de ce qui arrive sur terre n'est perdu pour le ciel. Tout y trouve son sens. Tout y est devenu explicable, la même chose maintenant intelligible» (*T*, II, 575).

This view of reality is of course the product of Claudel's religious beliefs. Faith, he tells us, lends a symbolic character to each one of our actions. «Rien ne se passe plus isolément, mais au regard d'une réalité supérieure» (*T*, II, 1414). For the Christian, life is not an incoherent series of incomplete gestures, but rather a precise drama with direction and meaning. Historical events parallel, illustrate and typify spiritual events. The visible universe is linked to the invisible through a mysterious tie which Claudel identifies with the relationship implied in an analogy. (I might add at this point that the discovery of the analogy, which suggests profound, secret relationships that are not rational or logical but rather intuitive, was an important occasion for Claudel. He states: «L'idée de l'analogie, l'idée dont saint Bonaventure donne la formule, ... est peut-être encore plus riche de conséquences au point de vue de la découverte que le syllogisme aristotelicien» [*Mi,* 156].)

In the first two chapters of this study we sensed how these ideas were present in Claudel's works. In Chapter I we learned that women for him always represent either Sophia, Mary, the Church, or the soul. We also became aware of the voluptuousness of his religious concepts. In keeping with this, it was suggested in Chapter II that man's relationship with woman bore some similarity to his bond with God. We saw how in Claudel's view surrender to woman and surrender to God require similar abandonment, how the phenomenon of rebirth is tied in with both relationships, and how the cross comes into play in both spheres.

In this chapter, I would like to continue to explore these similarities for, in effect, Claudel did say that there is only one love—but with diverse objects. «L'amour de Dieu», he explains, «fait appel en nous à la même faculté que celui des créatures, à ce sentiment qu'à nous seuls nous ne sommes pas complets et que le Bien suprême en qui nous serons réalisés est, hors de nous quelqu'un. Mais Dieu seul est cette réalité dont les créatures ne sont que l'image» (*Opr,* 431). Human love, the union of man and woman is then a shadow, an image —however humble or distorted—of divine love, the union of the soul and God. Claudel feels that he can confidently make this assertion for he knows that God is love and that in all which is love there is something present that resembles Him. In the love relationship «ce que nous donnons l'un à l'autre c'est Dieu sous des espèces différentes» (*Opo,* 687).

To support his claim Claudel also points out that in Scripture human love always serves as a figure of divine love. And this the poet avers is not simply a rhetorical device, but rather a substantive and deliberate relationship or analogy which holds true even down to the smallest detail, through all the nuances and vicissitudes of the poignant Biblical drama of love. We know of the symbolic erotic content of the Song of Songs, for instance. Claudel also notes that all of Israel's betrayals are depicted by the prophets as a form of prostitution or adultery. In keeping with this he himself refers to original sin as a form of incest—preference of oneself to God. «La Créature, / Voyant l'être qui lui était remis, s'en saisit, / Faisant d'elle-même sa fin, et tel fut le premier rapt et le premier inceste» (T, I, 824).

It might be further posited that this drama is constantly being relived by men and women today who re-enact the divine parable. This of course is reflected in Claudel's theatre. We saw how his female characters are identified with certain Scriptural figures. (To the list mentioned above we can add Eve, the Shulamite, Delilah, and Bathsheba.) We also went on to learn that for Claudel marriage was in the image of Calvary and the Mass, and passion was intimately associated with the cross, with the Passion. Claudel speaks of his object in writing *Partage de midi* in the following manner: «Ce ne sont point les passions que je veux peindre mais la *passion* d'une malheureuse âme» (T, I, 1334). It is not in vain, he tells us, that this phenomenon of human love in crisis carries the same name as the focal reality of Christian faith: Passion.

But how are these two experiences similar? To begin with we know that sexual penetration is linked with death and rebirth. In fact, Claudel notes that «la seconde de la conception salutifère est aussi impénétrable que celle de la conception sexuelle» (Oc, XXII, 426). Furthermore, sexual pleasure is said to be an allusion to the Eden which was lost and has been repromised. For an instant, the lovers cross over into that realm by way of the humiliation and death symbolized in the sex act.

On another level, we find St. Augustine making the following analysis which also elucidates the analogy: «Like a bridegroom Christ went forth from his chamber, he went out with a presage of his nuptuals into the field of the world. ... He came to the marriage bed of the cross, and there, in mounting it, he consummated his marriage. And when he perceived the sighs of the creature, he lovingly gave himself up to the torment in the place of his bride, ... and he joined the woman to himself forever» (1). This is reflected in Claudel's theatre by Rodrigue who cries out to Prouhèze: «Cette croix, mon amour, cette croix nue, cette croix déserte, c'est la couche, toi et moi, qui nous était réservée! C'est le lit nuptial, toi et moi, qui nous était réservé» (T, II, 1098).

Taking those remarks into account, we might add that these two experiences—the Passion of Christ and the passion of the lover—are also similar because of the suffering attendant to both. In the love situation, as in the Passion, this suffering is the necessary result of a sacrifice required—a sacrifice which is explained in the following passage: «Il y a un profond mystère et une source infinie de tragique dans le fait que nous sommes l'un à l'autre la condition du salut éternel, que nous portons en nous, nous seuls, la clef de l'âme de tel ou tel de nos frères qui ne peut être sauvé que par nous, et à nos propres dépens» (T, II, 1480). So when Prouhèze asks Camille if she must give up her life to save his, he answers that there is no other way.

In this connection Claudel also has said: «Toute rose pour moi est peu au prix de son épine! / Peu de chose est pour moi l'amour où manque la souffrance divine!» (T, I, 407). For divine suffering has far-reaching consequences. In L'Histoire de Tobie et de Sara the bramble tells us: «Sans ma fibre autour de son front, il n'aurait point de couronne!» (T, II, 1544). There is no victory without suffering, no new birth without the pangs of delivery. (In fact, the travail of this world may be seen in that light. Claudel explains: «Toute

---

(1) St. Augustine, *Sermo suppositus*, 120, 8 cited by Carl G. Jung, *Mysterium Coniunctionis*, trans. by R. F. C. Hull, 2nd ed., Bollingen Series XX (Princeton: Princeton University Press, 1968), p. 32.

la souffrance qu'il y a en ce monde, ce n'est pas la douleur de l'agonie, c'est celle de la parturition» [*Opr,* 811].)

We see then that in Claudel's view the divine plan calls for us all to relive Christ's Passion through love. But first the wounding must occur. And we hear Pensée cry: «C'est moi qui l'ai blessé, de cette blessure inguérissable. / C'est moi qui lui ai fendu la poitrine, / C'est moi qui lui ai ouvert la côte. / C'est moi qui l'ai arraché à son Père, oui je sais que c'est à cause de moi qu'il est mort et qu'il n'est plus rien de visible» (*T,* II, 565). Claudel tells us that Orian sacrifices his life for Pensée, who on one level represents Israel and on another, woman or the soul. It is for her and because of her that the sacrifice is made. (Small wonder then that Orian feared involvement with her. She did indeed represent danger and death.) So we see that in *Le Père humilié* we have been presented with a re-enactment of the Passion—followed by the Resurrection, for in the last act Orian's life reawakens in Pensée's breast.

It is, however, in *Partage de midi* that the divine drama is perhaps most fully relived. In the first act of this play we feel as though we had been taken back to the beginning of time. Amalric speaks of «la situation / Réduite à ses traits premiers, comme aux jours de la Création» (*T,* I, 1153). Ysé adds to the picture by telling us: «Il n'y a plus de ciel, il n'y a plus de mer, il n'y a plus que le néant, et au milieu épouvantable cette espèce d'animal fossile qui va se mettre à braire! ... Le brontosaure qui va se mettre à braire!» (*T,* I, 1176). Mesa also contributes to this impression when he describes the nature of his personal experience in the following manner: «En moi le profond dérangement / De la création, comme la Terre / Lorsque l'écume aux lèvres elle produisait la chose aride, et que dans un rétrécissement effroyable / Elle faisait sortir sa substance et le repli des monts comme de la pâte!» (*T,* I, 1027).

Then amid talk of pagan deities—Brahma, Lakshmi, Baal, Apollo—and of primitive sacrifices, the parable begins to unfold. Reference is made to Adam and Eve—Ysé mentions

Adam's sleep and Eve's creation. And Act II, we discover, takes place in an old Chinese cemetery which is called «ce jardin maudit». This of course brings to mind the Garden of Eden. We must add, however, that it also suggests the Garden of Gethsemane. It is here that Mesa as the first man Adam will sin (his sin is David's trespass—De Ciz is his Uriah), but it is also here that Mesa as the second Adam will contemplate union with his bride. This is undoubtedly symbolized by the eclipse which according to Christian tradition represents the mystic marriage or union of God with the human soul, with His Church, accomplished by Christ through His death on the cross.

Finally, in Act III we have the betrayal—the betrayal which imposes the sacrifice. (I should perhaps note at this point that through her infidelity Ysé aligns herself with many Biblical figures—perhaps most conspicuously with Delilah, but also with Eve whose unfaithfulness to God introduced sin and thereby occasioned the sacrifice, or with God's people who perpetuated and aggravated the breach through their disloyalty. These are all feminine figures representing God's beloved, the human soul, who necessitated the holocaust and for love of whom it was made.) It is then this betrayal which permits Mesa to say:

> Ah! je sais maintenant
> Ce que c'est que l'amour! Et je sais ce que vous
> avez enduré sur votre croix, dans ton coeur,
> Si vous avez aimé chacun de nous
> Terriblement comme j'ai aimé cette femme, et le
> râle, et l'asphyxie et l'étau!
> ... ...
> Trahi! Trahi! ... et vous savez de quelle soif, ô Dieu,
> Et sécheresse et horreur et extraction
> Je m'étais saisi d'elle! Et on nous a fait cela!
> Ah! vous vous y connaissez, vous savez, vous,
> Ce que c'est que l'amour trahi! (*T*, I, 1136).

This death and sacrifice result of course in eternal life for both Mesa and Ysé as they did for Christ and the soul or the Church. That being the case, we are not surprised to learn that in an early manuscript Claudel associates his personal experiences with the mystery of the Mass. In a text which Moriaki Watanabé labels ms. C we discover the following lines: «L'homme dans la splendeur de *la Messe* d'Août, l'Esprit vainqueur dans la Transfiguration de Midi!» (2). It is then true that we witness a re-enactment of the Passion in this play. We have indeed been presented with a parable of the divine plan.

It would seem appropriate now, I think, to consider the fact, which may be troublesome to some, that Claudel's parable is based upon an adulterous love affair. We ask ourselves how he could construct a parable of this nature around an illicit relationship. We soon discover, however, that an answer to this question cannot be discerned without first examining the Claudelian view of sin and evil.

Claudel goes to great lengths to expound the theory of *privatio boni,* a theory which seems to rob evil of all concrete reality by positing that it is merely the absence of good. The angel in *Soulier de satin* says: «Le mal est ce qui n'existe pas» (*T,* II, 819). Elsewhere Claudel reaffirms this by adding: «Le mal n'a pas d'existence par lui-même» (*Oc,* XV, 203). This of course ties in with his famous saying: «Le mal ne compose pas». In practice, however, Claudel, like most of us, treats evil as an independent reality and ascribes a very interesting role to it in the providential economy. This role is described as follows: «Le mal sert, la souffrance sert, le péché sert, l'enfer sert, tout cela a coopéré à cette croix» (*Oc,* XXI, 444). Satan, we learn, has been reduced to the position of unconscious ally in God's plan. «Le Mal est dans le monde comme un esclave qui fait monter l'eau» (*T,* I, 848). Hell itself must pay homage to God. So, without losing anything of his execrable character, the devil is permitted

---

(2) Moriaki Watanabé, «Le 'Don', ou la logique dramatique de *Partage de midi*», *La Revue des Lettres Modernes,* Nos. 180-82 (1968), 46.

to serve. As Mesa says: «Le mal même / Comporte son bien qu'il ne faut pas laisser perdre» (*T*, I, 1057). Claudel goes on to add: «La croix est l'hameçon et Satan maintenant lui-même lui sert d'amorce! Nous n'avalerons jamais Satan si profond que nous n'avalions en même temps cet hameçon qui lui est incorporé» (*Oc*, XIX, 278-79). This is why the Jesuit father in *Soulier de satin* was able to pray for Rodrigue in the following manner: «Il n'est pas si facile de Vous échapper, et s'il ne va pas à Vous par ce qu'il a de clair, qu'il y aille par ce qu'il a d'obscur» (*T*, II, 668). Christ, we discover, administers this darkness and has put it at the service of His elect.

So we see that although we are obviously not permitted to seek the good through evil means, should we happen to stumble into evil God has the power of making it work for the good, thereby actually transforming it into good. As Claudel tells us, God is «un être économe qui se sert de tout» (*Mi*, 216). (In fact, this, he feels, is one of the proofs of Providence.)

Keeping all of these things in mind, let us now turn our attention to Claudel's views regarding evil in the Biblical drama, for here we will see how he develops the theory that sin not only serves in God's plan but is actually necessary to it. He begins by telling us that the fruit of the tree of the knowledge of good and of evil carried within it the seed of redemption. He then goes on to echo Church liturgy by exclaiming: *Felix Culpa! Heureuse faute! très nécessaire péché!* It was through sin that redemption was procured. It was with sin that a new world appeared—the world of penance. Sin was the necessary irritant, the necessary provocation which produced the divine reaction that yielded salvation through sacrifice.

It is not surprising that one of Claudel's favorite Biblical stories was the tale of David and Bathsheba. And it is fascinating to note the importance he attributes to this episode the circumstances of which so closely resemble his own love story. He says: «Paix à toi, Bethsabée! Paix à cette femme qui a labouré David et qui a enfin obtenu de lui ces cris profondément ensevelis au coeur de l'homme auxquels l'oreille de Dieu depuis le jour de la Faute était vainement attentive!» (*Oc,* XXIII, 343). Everything began with Bathsheba, he asserts. «Ne Lui fallait-il obtenir Salomon?» (*Oc,* XXIV, 119) from whose lineage Jesus sprang. But what of Uriah? And Claudel retorts: «Tant pis pour Urias!» (*Oc,* XXIII, 349).

Sin, we learn, is like disease. Just as in the physical realm disease makes us aware of our bodies, so in the spiritual realm sin heightens our consciousness. The moral man who obeys all the laws enjoys only a negative peace. He lives in a state of somnolence. Sin will introduce the necessary jolt to hurl him into the world of penance. It will break him and reduce him to himself (as was the case with David).

To further emphasize his point of view the poet also makes the following remark: «À prendre les paroles sacrées à la lettre, on croirait même que l'amour de Dieu pour nous s'accroît à proportion de nos fautes, qu'Il nous est reconnaissant de cette croix pour qu'Il y trouve habitation, puisqu'elle exclut de Lui à nous la séparation, que nous ne cessons chaque jour de Lui menuiser!» (*Oc,* XXIII, 347). He also reminds us that St. Paul speaks not only of the utility but also of the necessity of heresies—«la négation formant comme un écran qui oblige à se dessiner une vérité diffuse» (*Oc,* XXV, 532).

If we turn to Claudel's theatre we also find much that reaffirms this conviction. In *L'Échange* Marthe says of Louis: «C'était un innocent avant qu'il ne m'ait connue! C'est moi qui lui ai appris le péché. Il le fallait» (*T,* I, 773). (Curiously enough this «sin» is union with her on the marriage bed.) Claudel adds that it was through and because of this union (which he has labeled sin) that Louis was able to pass over into the realm of prayer. Similarly, in *Soulier de satin* Musique remarks: «Il fallait la nuit pour que cette lampe apparaisse, il fallait tout ce bouleversement ... / Pour que, fermant les yeux, je trouve en moi mon enfant, cette simple

— 65 —

petite vie qui commence!» (*T*, II, 786). And in *L'Histoire de Tobie et de Sara* the angel asks Tobie: «N'étais-je pas là même pour t'égarer quand il le fallait?» (*T*, II, 1291).

In Claudel's view the path to light is of necessity through darkness and so we find many examples of good coming from evil in his plays. In addition to those cited above we might also mention the fact that the white dove in *Le Livre de Christophe Colomb* was a present to Isabelle from the Sultan Miramolin. We also know of the good wrought by Mara and Camille. «Ochiali le Renégat a rendu plus de services au Roi d'Espagne que Don Camille le bailli» (*T*, II, 850), affirms Prouhèze. He also demanded a sacrifice which led to salvation, as did Mara.

All of this should serve to explain why Claudel felt that his experience with sin could serve as a parable of the divine drama. (We should also note that Claudel went so far as to state that his conversion did not transform him essentially. It was his passion that broke him, thereby releasing new life.)

To some critics Claudel's claim that his love experience was in keeping with God's will for his life and that through it he somehow relived the Fall and the Redemption, smacks of unconscious sophistry. Howells, for instance, writes: «It was this kind of unconscious sophistry where the status of passion is concerned which enabled Claudel in Act III of *Partage de midi* to hold up adulterous passion as a form of the soul's longing for God. More important than that; it enables the Mesa of Act II to experience all the anguish of remorse and guilt without ever really acknowledging responsibility» (3). He also affirms that this unconscious dishonesty led to Claudel's convictions regarding the fatality of the incident.

To some extent what Howells says is undoubtedly true.

_____

(3) Howells, «The enigma of *Partage de midi*», in *Claudel: A Reappraisal*, p. 31.

Yet, we must keep in mind the fact that Claudel's feelings of fatality, for instance, appear to have been present in the relationship from the start. It does not then seem to me that these feelings of entrapment stemmed from an unconscious effort to shirk responsability for his behavior, but rather from the unconscious phenomenon of fascination which we are told is always accompanied by these reactions. Furthermore, one must concede that Claudel did accept responsability to the extent that he was able to say: «Notre liberté bien entendu reste intacte, jamais nous ne nous en sommes aussi bien aperçus. Mais grand Dieu, pourquoi est-ce à ce moment précis qu'il s'est offert à nous ce visage de femme?» (T, II, 1499).

Another point can also be made on his behalf. The fact that Claudel as early as 1886 already identified his female characters with God's Wisdom indicates that as of that date he already linked the human love experience with the soul's longing for God. It is then impossible to claim that he devised his notions on passion to relieve himself of accountability for his actions, for those actions had not yet taken place when he formulated his theories. As some critics have said, throughout much of Claudel's theatre—particularly in the plays written prior to 1900—the intervention of woman (or l'Autre) is symbolic of the divine intervention—the intrusion of Sophia in the poet's life. Jacques Petit, for instance, makes the following comments concerning La Ville: «On a remarqué depuis longtemps ... que la rencontre de Coeuvre et de Thalie traduisait dramatiquement la conversion de Claudel» (4). We also know that the Princess in Tête d'Or can easily be identified with Sophia. When we hear Claudel say: «Depuis ma conversion, ... je n'ai cessé de voir dans la femme une image (ou une caricature) de la Sagesse divine. Mais la Sagesse divine repoussée par les hommes» (Opr, 467),

---

(4) Jacques Petit, «La structure», in «La première version de La Ville», La Revue des Lettres Modernes, Nos. 209-11. (1969), 44.

the Princess' lament immediately comes to mind: «Il me faut, céans, / Partir seule comme une veuve chassée durement de la maison!» (*T, I, 66*). (Note that use of the word *veuve* imparts sexual overtones to the relationship at hand.) All of this obviates much of Howells' criticism although it still might be contended that Claudel's views on sin were indeed rather complacent.

Returning to our original object—to explore the the similarities between human and divine love relationships—we should now add that in Claudel's universe these two relationships also resemble each other in the amount of violence inherent to both. He tells us: «Il n'y a pas de fécondation sans amour et il n'y a pas d'amour sans violence» (*Oc, XXIV, 464*). Just as he speaks of human love in terms of conquest, he also puts divine love into that same context. When Rodrigue remarks: «L'Esprit parle, le désir parle, c'est bien. / En avant! il n'y a plus qu'à lui obéir aussitôt», Camille adds: «Il n'y a pas d'autre moyen de conquérir le salut dans l'autre monde et les femmes dans celui-ci» (*T, II, 771*). We also hear Orso say of Orian: «Ce Dieu qu'il aimait comme un sauvage et non pas comme un saint, il l'a conquis» (*T, II, 564*). And we find Mesa described as a conquering hero at the end of *Partage de midi*. He is «l'Esprit vainqueur dans la transformation de Midi» (*T, I, 1139*). In keeping with this Claudel describes his relationship with God in the following terms: «Nous sommes constitués ensemble non pas dans l'inertie et dans la mort, mais dans cet amour que j'appellerai absurdement un antagonisme inépuisable. Jamais je ne viendrai à bout de mon ennemi» (*Oc, XXII, 193*). But neither will he willingly succumb: «O Dieu, ni devant les hommes, ni devant toi, / Je ne baisserai point les yeux. C'est moi! / C'est moi! Il me faut vaincre ou mourir sur la place» (*Opo, 17*).

Claudel is fond of calling to mind the fact that Christ said He came to bring the sword, war, division, separation, and not peace. (The poet ties this in with the positive nature of violence as described in Chapter II.) He also reminds us that Jesus said that the kingdom of heaven suffered violence. Claudel seems to interpret this latter remark to mean that God can be «forced» into doing certain things —answering prayer, for instance. He points out how most of the prayers reported in the Gospels consist of daring demands. They entail a struggle, almost a conflict between man's will and the divine will. This violent attitude is reflected in many of Claudel's characters—Georges, Sara, Camille, and Mara of whom it is said: «L'impitoyable foi, l'impitoyable nécessité de Mara, et sous l'exigence irrésistible, le droit sur Dieu, la victoire sur Dieu, la puissance sur Dieu, qui s'éveille du fond d'un être dévoré» (*T*, II, 1389). Camille illustrates how Claudel feels that sin can «force» God into action, just as it did in the divine drama. He exclaims: «Et moi, je vais être si malheureux et si criminel, oui, je vais faire de telles choses, Doña Prouhèze, / Que je vous forcerai bien à venir à moi, vous et ce Dieu que vous gardez si jalousement pour vous, comme s'il était venu pour les justes» (*T*, II, 676-77).

Eventually, however, the divine will triumphs (despite appearances to the contrary) and man must submit—be it with dignity («Et je fus devant vous comme un lutteur qui plie, / Non qu'il se croie faible, mais parce que l'autre est plus fort» [*Opo*, 249].) or in humiliation («J'ai fui en vain: partout j'ai trouvé la Loi. / Il faut céder enfin! ô porte, il faut admettre / L'hôte; coeur frémissant, il faut subir le maître» [*Opo*, 18]). This submission is of course mirrored by the submission required in the human love relationship.

Now we might ask: What of the dangers woman represents? Do these somehow correspond to analogous spiritual threats? The answer is undoubtedly yes, or why else would *le deuxième consacré* in *La Ville* hand the king a sword and say: «Prends-la, ô Roi, et défends-nous, / Je dis contre Dieu, afin qu'il nous attende avec patience» (*T*, I, 413). For as we see in *Le Festin de la Sagesse* man can be forced into God's kingdom. Disease, war, poverty, and woman are the divine goads. And it must be said that the danger presented here seems to lend a frightening, ambiguous quality to the Deity. This ambiguity is reflected in Sophia, God's Wisdom, who as Judith wields a lethal knife and is called «la dangereuse Sagesse de Dieu». It can also be discerned in the omega image in *Partage de midi.* The omega obviously symbolizes God who said: «I am the Alpha and the Omega, the beginning and the ending» (5). Yet it is also variously called *trou, piège,* and *trône nuptial* in this play. This same ambiquity is also apparent in an episode from *L'Histoire de Tobie et de Sara*—the episode in which Tobie encounters a fish (symbolic of Christ) with whom he struggles. Tobie fears the fish will devour him. But instead, it proves to be Tobie's salvation. It transports him across the river and then gives of its flesh for Tobie's nourishment.

Perhaps the image that best depicts the ambiguous nature of human intercourse with the Deity is fire. «Je suis le feu!» affirms God's Grace. «Qui M'a touché, / Il faut qu'il consente à brûler» (*Opo,* 816-17). Christ Himself said He came to earth to bring fire—a fire which Claudel describes as «un feu latent, un feu souterrain, qui ... ne cessera point de travailler l'humanité» (*Oc,* XXIII, 306); a fire (symbolic of His Holy Spirit) that illumines, penetrates, softens and welds, that consumes and consummates, spiritualizes and purifies, that destroys everything in us which is not immortal. As Claudel tells us: «C'est seulement quand Il nous aura bien débarbouillés avec ce feu, au jour du Jugement, que le Père en nous reconnaîtra Son oeuvre» (*Oc,* XXIII, 418). This is God's devouring flame which is the delight of his saints and the torment of the damned. «Ce même feu qui nourrit en vous la vie / Dans le ciel est des êtres bienheureux la splendeur et la fusion / Qui de l'Enfer est la passion et la brûlure» (*T,* I, 827). It is the instrument through which God manifests Himself and communicates with man. It is the fire which consumed Violaine and in which Jeanne d'Arc

---

(5) Revelations 1:8.

was sacrificed. Claudel says of this martyr: «Elle embrasse l'holocauste. Cette flamme dont on la menaçait, elle s'y jette volontairement. Ce n'est pas assez dire qu'elle l'accepte, elle l'épouse» (*T,* II, 1526). Prouhèze also came into contact with it and cried: «Non, non, ne me sépare plus à jamais de ces flammes désirées! Il faut que je leur donne à fondre et à dévorer cette carapace affreuse, ... tout cela que Dieu n'a pas fait, tout ce roide bois d'illusion et de péché, cette idole, cette abominable poupée que j'ai fabriquée à la place de l'image vivante de Dieu dont ma chair portait le sceau empreint!» (*T,* II, 822). This is a fire which can only grow at the expense of the vessel which supports its flame. It destroys what gives it nourishment and what it cannot destroy it softens.

But what of the flame of passionate human love? What connection is there between this fire and the one described above? Our answer is contained in the following definition. Fire, we are told, is «la forme extérieure et la vertu intime de l'amour» (*Oc,* XIX, 131). It is then a manifestation of God's love and with its full destructive potential it is also the image of human love and sexual desire. Claudel states: «Ce côté destructeur de l'Amour divin [le feu] et dont tant de Saints ont été la proie, l'Amour humain lui aussi nous apporte souvent l'image, dégradée tant qu'on voudra, mais terrifiante, de sa puissance pénétrante et irrésistible» (*Oc,* XXII, 185). It is said of Ysé and Mesa: «[Ils] se demandent l'un à l'autre cet élément, cet aliment intérieur que l'on appelle le feu, et que la créature n'usurpe à son usage que pour sa propre destruction. Au lieu de les illumi-ner, il les brûle. Au lieu de les consommer, il les consume» (*T,* I, 1339). This is the nature of human passion which is illicit. The lovers, like Prometheus, would steal God's fire, divert it from its proper function, only to be devoured by it in the end as Prometheus was devoured by the vulture. This guilty passion is referred to as *le feu rouge, le feu sombre* or *la grande flamme noire.* Mesa says to Ysé: «Je lis enfin, et j'en ai horreur, dans tes yeux le grand appel panique! /

Derrière tes yeux qui me regardent la grande flamme noire de l'âme qui brûle de toutes parts comme une cité dévorée! / La sens-tu bien maintenant dans ton sein, la mort de l'amour et le feu que fait un coeur qui s'embrase?» (*T*, I, 1027).

But let us be reminded that the burning flames of this love wreak a necessary and salutary destruction of the individual, as was the case with Mesa and Rodrigue. They both were broken by their love. So we see that this *feu rouge,* the fire of human passion, can serve, it can lead to salvation, but only through sacrifice—the sacrifice or destruction of self necessary to the redemptive process.

Let us now continue our investigation by examining still other ways in which the union of man and woman serves as an allegory of God's union with humanity. In Chapter II of this study it was mentioned that the relationship between the sexes in Claudel's universe could be compared to the relationship between hunter and hunted. Now we go on to observe that the Claudelian lovers are possessed of a desire to feed on one another. This is evidenced in numerous plays. In *L'Otage,* for instance, we hear Georges tell Sygne: «[J'] ai vraiment faim et soif de ton coeur hors de moi» (*T*, II, 236). Similarly, in *Partage de midi* Mesa describes his sensual desire as follows: «Je suis comme un affamé qui ne peut retenir ses larmes à la vue de la nourriture!» (*T*, I, 1022). Elsewhere Ysé says: «O ineffable iniquité! Ah viens donc et mange-moi comme une mangue!» (*T*, I, 1026). She then speaks of Mesa's cruel teeth in her heart and of his devouring eyes. Amalric refers to Ysé's lovers in these terms: «Et le dernier amant, / Comme un fruit que l'on a fini de manger, et l'on s'essuie la bouche, il y reste encore comme un petit goût» (*T*, I, 1036). And finally Mesa adds: «Qu'y a-t-il en toi que tu ne m'aies / Donné, et que je n'aie eu, et mangé, et aspiré, et qui ne me nourrisse de feu, et de larmes, et de désespoir!» (*T*, I, 1046). In *L'Échange* Marthe also expresses herself in a kindred manner: «Je te donnais mon coeur à manger / Comme un fruit où les dents restent enfoncées» (*T*, I, 721). And in *La Muse qui est la Grâce* human passion is spoken of in this fashion: «Qui a mordu à la terre, il en conserve le goût entre les dents. / Qui a goûté le sang, il ne se nourrira plus d'eau brillante et de miel ardent! ... Quelque chose de lui-même désormais hors de lui vit au pain d'un autre corps» (*Opo*, 276). The love experience is also linked to eating in *Le Repos du septième jour:* «Assouvissement comme de la nourriture; satisfaction, comme la jonction de l'homme avec la femme!» (*T,* I, 860).

In an attempt to explain this association of ideas, Claudel tells us that the religious commandment «love one another» has more to do with the commandment of nature «eat one another» than one would suspect. «Dieu sait la mauvaise littérature qui s'est déchaînée sur la prétendue férocité de la nature, sur le scandale de ces êtres qui se dévorent les uns les autres. Mais s'ils se dévorent, c'est qu'ils s'aiment, c'est qu'ils ont besoin l'un de l'autre, c'est qu'ils ne peuvent se passer l'un de l'autre, c'est qu'ils appartiennent l'un à l'autre» (*Opr,* 988). Claudel also speaks of «cette loi fondamentale de la nature que les créatures ne puissent se passer les unes des autres et qu'elles s'aiment jusqu'à la dévoration. Pourquoi ne pas y voir une forme élémentaire de la communion» (*Oc,* XXI, 355). With this we can envisage the religious overtones of this phenomenon.

The theme of eating, which has thus far been overlooked by the critics, is one of considerable import in Claudel's works. It appears repeatedly in a most provocative manner. Claudel speaks, for instance, of «la lumière comestible» (*Oc,* XXI, 224). Humanity, we are told, is in search of an edible truth (*Oc,* XXI, 473). The Bible is a thing to be eaten, to be digested (*Oc,* XXI, 11). God sends us Grace in mouthfuls suited to the size of our mouths and our ability to assimilate (*Oc,* XIX, 152). We also discover that before the marvel of God and His creation our whole being is like a mouth which opens to encompass and absorb (*Oc,* XXV, 241). Then Claudel tells us of the nutritive inefficaciousness of all that has attempted to replace Catholicism. «L'estomac ne prend point le change» (*Opr,* 778-79). Finally, we find that many of his female characters are identified with edible substances. Sara says she is the fruit, the wine, the bread, the fig, the pomegranate. Violaine is also compared to fruit and bread—the bread of which one does not tire. (We can explain the epithet «douce-amère» which is often used to describe women—Marthe, in particular—by recalling two remarks made by the poet. In the first, he tells us that the Gospel is sweet in our mouths but bitter when swallowed because it wars against our depraved nature [Oc, XXVI, 68]. In the second, we learn that the book the angels gave John to eat in the Apocalypse was sweet to his mouth but bitter in his stomach because he had not received it to keep [Oc, XXII, 199]. It might then be concluded that woman is bittersweet for the same reasons. She is sweet to the senses, but bitter in a more profound manner. Her spirituality makes bitter demands upon man—she requires sacrifice and denial as did Violaine and Marthe—and her sensuality, which often leads to unfaithfulness, imposes a bitter sharing. Such was the case with Ysé.)

As we learned from the passage cited above, this theme derives its significance in Claudel's works from the sacrament of Holy Communion during which it might be said that the believer is united with Christ and nourished by Him. It is because of the nature of this sacrament, because «le principe de la manducation ... est consommé dans l'Eucharistie» (J, I, 370) that Claudel is able to say that all nourishment should be an offering, that «la table de famille en effet n'est pas une mangeoire, c'est une espèce d'autel qui aspire à culminer dans autre chose que la satisfaction de notre besoin animal» (Opr, 358). (In Annonce faite à Marie the family table is actually transformed into a sacrificial altar.) During the celebration of the Eucharist, Christ is sacrificed and then resurrected in the transformed substances. Man's participation in this rite is described as follows by Claudel: «Le tombeau où le Christ ... est mis, / Ce n'est pas seulement ce sépulcre neuf, c'est ma chair, / C'est l'homme, votre créature, qui est plus profond que la terre!» (Opo, 487). He also says: «Nos mâchoires

... sont un sépulcre ouvert et c'est seulement quand on lui aura fourni la nourriture qu'elle réclame que notre *terre* trouvera le repos» (*Oc*, XXIV, 192). (This mystery is irreverently mirrored in a remark made by Balthazar in *Le Soulier de satin:* «Ce pâté comme un sépulcre de chaires embaumées sous de puissantes épices pour ressusciter dans l'estomac avec une chaleur bienfaisante!» [*T*, II, 722]. It also serves to explain the fairy tale told by Violaine in the first version of *La Jeune Fille Violaine*. The precious stone with its transforming powers is symbolic of Christ who in the Apocalypse is a white pebble that we are given to ingest.) So it might be said that through eating man participates in the redemptive act, just as through eating he fell from Grace in the Garden of Eden.

It is this mystery which is dimly reflected in the lovers' desperate attempts at union in the sexual embrace. «Dans le transport de l'amour humain, qui ne sait qu'on se mange, qu'on se dévore, qu'on voudrait s'incorporer en toutes manières, et, comme disait un poète, enlever jusqu'avec les dents ce qu'on aime, pour le posséder, pour s'en nourrir, pour s'y unir, pour en vivre?» (6). For we know that there is no perfect delectation, no real possession other than that which is procured by absorbing the object of our desire, by assimilating it, by disappearing in it and it in us. The activity of the lovers is naturally to this end, but they soon discover that this effort to attain spiritual union through physical means is futile. As Mesa says: «Cela qui nous tient séparés, ... la chose qui refuse, et qui sépare et qui dit non, / Ce n'est pas ... avec des morsures que l'on en vient à bout, c'est avec la croix!» (*T*, I, 1221).

It is only through sacrifice—the sacrifice of human love and the transcendance into divine love—that spiritual union is feasible; for what is fury and impotence in human passion

---

(6) Jacques-Bénigne Bossuet, *Méditations sur l'Évangile*, cited by Claudel, *J*, I, 264.

is truth and wisdom in Jesus' love. This is why we are told that union is possible—that we are edible—only to the degree to which we have been sanctified through sacrifice. Or as Claudel puts it: «La sainteté d'un homme ne réside-t-elle pas dans la mesure où il est mangeable, approprié à la communion?» (*Opr*, 988). It is for this reason that Violaine is called a beautiful ripe fruit whereas Mara is a winter nut, «amère au dehors, dur au dedans comme une pierre» (*T*, I, 640). We also know that the nuns of Monsanvierge—those living sacrifices—are likened to Hosts. It is through sacrifice that we are transformed into Christ's image—«le Christ mangeable»—in whom Claudel affirms «il n'y a rien ... que nous n'aimions, qui ne nous soit mangeable» (*Oc*, XXII, 226). Through sacrifice we are exposed to God's devouring flame and made holy. We are consecrated. «Ce que nous lui sacrifions, Il le consacre. Il achève le pain et le vin» (*T*, II, 271). («Le vin que font une âme et un corps mis ensemble sous le pressoir» [*Opo*, 515].)

We have said that spiritual union cannot be achieved through the sexual intercourse of two bodies or through the oral activity described above. But now let us hasten to add that it somehow can be attained through another type of oral contact. And here we encounter the importance of the kiss. In *Tête d'Or*, Simon Agnel speaks of this taction in the following terms: «Nous avons réuni nos âmes par la bouche» (*T*, I, 174). We also know of the importance attributed to the kiss in *L'Annonce faite à Marie*. It was following this type of union that Violaine was said to have conceived the suffering of the world and Pierre was able to give birth to his churches. They were both made spiritually fertile through this contact. Lechy speaks of a spiritual seed when she remarks: «Mais je porte dans la chaleur de ma bouche une dissolution plus parfaite, ... / Et ils ne s'approchent de moi en vain; mais ils emportent de moi de la semence» (*T*, I, 705). (Elsewhere the poet says: «J'ai ensemencé ta bouche de baisers» [*J*, I, 372].) We also see conception linked with oral activity in *Le Repos du septième jour*. It is said of the necromancer: «La pointe de la langue retournée contre le palais, il s'est conçu lui-même» (*T*, I, 805). Finally, in *Le Soulier de satin* we hear Prouhèze speak of «ce baiser tout à l'heure en qui nous avons été faits un seul!» (*T*, II, 779) and the Moon adds: «Son âme s'est séparé de lui dans ce baiser, ... Tout ce qui pouvait être donné, c'est fait» (*T*, II, 781). The evidence of spiritual union is of course the Double Shadow—which brings to mind the Overshadowing as a penetration which led to conception. (This is all reflected in the activities of the monks, described by Rodrigue, who exchanged the kiss of peace and in doing so «ils projettaient leurs ombres l'un sur l'autre» [*T*, II, 908]. Claudel speaks of the importance of the shadow and its link with conception in the following passage: «[Dieu] communique avec nous non pas par des paroles mais par son ombre qui nous couvre et nous remplit, ... Et alors à nous est réservé ce mystère d'une espèce de conception» [*T*, II, 440].)

But there are also other instances in which the importance of the mouth becomes apparent. Violaine, for example, says of the abbey's miller: «Plût à Dieu qu'il m'eût appelée quand sa femme était malade / Avec sa tumeur au sein, et qu'il m'eût laissée y mettre les lèvres!» (*T*, I, 536). It is also through a kiss that she restores sight to Aubin. Then in *Tête d'Or* the Princess exclaims: «Elle ne t'abandonnera pas celle que tu as délivrée en baisant ses mains sanglantes!» (*T*, I, 160). We also hear Lumîr say: «Mon âme, / Voici que je la leur apporte, comme un prisonnier lié par tous les membres, qui cherche son frère dans la nuit avec la bouche» (*T*, II, 476). Finally, we know that the Emperor in *Le Repos du septième jour* returns from Hell leprous, with everything consumed, burned, except his mouth.

And now we may ask why so much importance is attributed to the mouth and the kiss. How and why is it associated with conception? But before we can answer this question we should recall the circumstances surrounding the creation of Adam. We are told: «Then the Lord God formed man of dust from the ground, and breathed into his nostrils the breath of life; and man became a living being» (7). With this in mind let us now consider a passage from «O Rose éternelle» describing the relationship between the Virgin and her creator: «Elle exhale à la face de son créateur en restitution odorante de ce baiser jadis qui lui a né [sic] son âme» (*Oc,* XXV, 513). We see here how the kiss is connected with creation. We also learn, however, that it is intimately linked with breathing. Claudel speaks of «cet esprit que nous avons aspiré pour en faire notre vie de la bouche même de Dieu» (*Oc,* XX, 143). This is the kiss of life. This is the kiss Violaine gave Pierre («Violaine de bas en haut prend la tête de Pierre entre ses mains et lui aspire l'âme» [*T,* II, 145]), the kiss which typifies our relations with God and to which Claudel refers when he says: «Jamais je ne viendrai à bout de mon ennemi, jamais je ne cesserai de trouver bouche à bouche dans la verticale autre chose que cette raison de maintenir à jamais par rapport à elle l'extension sacrée de l'horizontale» (*Oc,* XXII, 193). Elsewhere we also find this contact with the Deity described in similar terms: «Le Dieu extérieur ... en un profond baiser se communique à ce Dieu intérieur en nous» (*Oc,* XXII, 377); «Leur conversation est avec l'Absolu, leur jonction avec l'Invariable, le baiser intérieur, dans le goût duquel ils s'abîment, lui-même» (*T,* I, 855). We also discover that Prouhèze speaks of «le néant à chaque moment où je sombre et Dieu sur ma bouche qui me ressuscite» (*T,* II, 821). So we see that the oral activity of Claudel's characters, and of man in general, mirrors an ever-present spiritual reality.

The importance of breathing in this union is of course vital. The soul is a breath-being and for that reason all true spiritual communication is connected with respiration. In *La Ville* it is said: «Que tu reçoives mon souffle et que j'aie avec toi communication... Et voici que je te possède et t'ai dans le souffle» (*T,* I, 446-47). In *L'Annonce faite à Marie*

---

(7) Genesis 2:7.

Violaine tells Jacques: «Est-ce que mon âme n'est pas assez? prends-la et je suis ici et aspire-la jusques aux racines qui est à toi!» (*T,* II, 54). We also know that Pensée breathed in Orso's mouth to communicate her soul to Orian and that she breathed Orian's soul in the flowers and life was given to their child. (At this point we should perhaps mention the perfume which we are told is contained in the innermost reaches of the heart. It is that eternal quality which is called the essence of the creature and is compared to the fragrance of a rose that gains strength as the flower dies. It is the odor «qui fait vivre les dieux» [*T,* II, 1251], the flavor of the soul, the fragrance which results from prayer and sacrifice.)

In *La Ville* we find it said: «Le Père et le Fils / S'étreignent dans l'unité de la Respiration» (*T,* I, 412). It is from the nature of this union, which is reflected in human ties, that breathing derives its significance. We might also add that our relationship with God naturally follows the same pattern. Frère Léon tells us that we have only to breathe to be filled with the divine presence. God delights in the sacred exhalation of all that exists. Spiritual rebirth is defined as a reopening to the breath that created us. And if we wonder about the afterlife, we are told that the saints in paradise «seront occupés à respirer Dieu et Dieu sera occupé à les respirer. À respirer leur âme et à la faire passer à l'intérieur de Lui-même, et eux à leur tour à respirer Son Esprit et à Le faire passer à l'interieur d'eux-mêmes» (*Oc,* XXIV, 454). Here we have the spiritual marriage of which the prophets and mystics spoke. This too will be the image of our relationship with our loved ones in the hereafter. We will absorb them in a single glance, a single breath.

We should also remark in this connection that the Holy Spirit who is called the breath and function of the Trinity is also intimately associated with fire. The link between fire and air is apparent. We know that air feeds and maintains fire. In terms of our own internal combustion this activity is described as follows: «[Le sang] puise sur l'autel de nos poumons, ... un feu lumineux» (*Oc,* XXVI, 46). On another level, this same relationship between fire and air is alluded to in *Soulier de satin* when the angel tells Prouhèze that God will breathe on her and she will become a flaming star in the breath of the Holy Spirit—a flaming sacrifice nourished by the divine breath. For the star in Claudel's universe is the product of sacrifice—the outward manifestation of sacrifice. It is a spiritual explosion, a divine holocaust.

This spiritual explosion, this divine holocaust is said to be the initial form and in a sense the supreme expression of union with God (just as fire is «cette forme suprême du souffle» [*Oc, XIX, 66*]). Claudel tells us that the soul in the presence of her creator «fait en quelque sorte explosion, lâchant, libérant, extrapolant, tout cet acquis, dont la vie a chargé sa conscience intérieure» (*Oc, XXII, 420*). This holocaust results from the fact that the soul in a state of supreme vibration has caught fire upon contact with the divine spark. (This is a phenomenon that is of course mirrored in the orgasm which we have already seen described as a detonation that abolishes time. It is, however, also reflected in the actual explosions that occur in Claudel's theatre which serve to unite the lovers.)

On another level, it is said that the fire which consumes His living sacrifices works to transform them into «parfum, esprit, essence, exhalaison» (*Oc, XXII, 160*). We are told: «J'ai mis Mes narines, J'ai mis Mon visage en plein dans la fumée de cet holocauste impur dans cette combustion de l'encens et de la graisse. Tout cela est à Moi pour que Je l'absorbe» (*Oc, XX, 109*).

This explains why Claudel calls fire a uniting force, how it is connected with air and breathing, and why he says that it is fire which gives us the means of penetrating into the depth of the Godhead. And if we keep in mind that fire is the exterior form and the interior quality of love, we will see that all of this also further elucidates that phenomenon.

CHAPTER IV

THE WORD

Mais il est une autre forme de sacrifice et d'holocauste plus parfaite encore, dont il est lui-même à la fois l'agent et l'autel et dont cette parole née du souffle que Dieu a fait passer dans son coeur et dans sa bouche est l'instrument.... C'est l'univers entier que nous inhalons par la contemplation et par l'intelligence et que nous restituons à Dieu après en avoir fait du chant, du sens et de l'esprit. D'un trait de nos poumons nous absorbons le monde, nous en remplissons notre coeur et nous en faisons cette parole musicale en quoi tout est consumé beaucoup plus parfaitement que la graisse sous l'action de la flamme (*Oc*, XXV, 539).

With this passage, which touches on many of the themes studied in Chapter III, we discern a new orientation for our continuing discussion of Claudel's works. Here for the first time we come into contact with his theories concerning «the word» and the creative process as it pertains to art or literary production. These are to be the subjects of this present chapter. So after having considered creativity in the spiritual realm, i.e., the creative process involved in spiritual rebirth, we will now study another type of creativity—the creativity of the artist. In so doing we will explore the importance Claudel attributes to «the word» and also determine what role woman and the feminine principle might have in this sphere.

As is readily apparent, in the above quotation Claudel mentions breathing and fire as well as sacrifice and explosion, and all of these motifs are connected with a verbal offering.

There is obviously much to be said about this passage, but perhaps the first and most important observation to be made is that in it we witness a merging of the priestly function with the role of poet. In it there emerges the figure of poet/priest, a figure which is not foreign to Claudel's universe, however. We know of Coeuvre in *La Ville,* for instance —a poet who later becomes bishop. And in *Le Soulier de satin* we hear it said: «Est-ce que toute cette beauté sera inutile? venue de Dieu, est-ce qu'elle n'est pas faite pour y revenir? Il faut le poète et le peintre pour l'offrir à Dieu, pour réunir un mot à l'autre mot et de tout ensemble faire action de grâces et reconnaisance et prière soustraite au temps» (*T,* II, 749).

As one might suspect, the merger of priestly and poetic functions described above is made possible by the nature of the Word—the Word who was made flesh. The importance of the verbal offering stems from His very identity as Word. Claudel exclaims: «L'avènement du Verbe! La délivrance de toutes les créatures par la parole, la libération en chacune d'elles de la parole qu'elle est et le verbe qui vient enfin sur elle s'ajouter au substantif» (*Opr,* 812). Elsewhere he also speaks of the Word «en qui tout est parole» (*Op,* 378).

In connection with this we should make special note of the pecularly verbal nature of Claudel's universe: Mesa tells us of his desire to be opened in the middle like a book, associating this experience, interestingly enough, with love: «O la joie d'être pleinement aimé! ô le désir de s'ouvrir par le milieu comme un livre!» (*T,* I, 1001). We know too that the Double Shadow in *Le Soulier de satin* refers to herself as «ce mot un instant hors de la terre lisible parmi ce pattement d'ailes éperdues» (*T,* II, 777). In «Cantate à trois voix» we read of «le moment d'où tout depend / Le mot suprême de l'année / De la terre qui désire encore et qui veut parler!» (*Opo,* 331). Claudel also speaks of the inspired author of Scriptures who compares our soul to a sheet of paper on which the Holy Spirit traces characters and signs. He is said to be addressing us missives.

Then there is the *book* of Joan of Arc of whom Claudel says: «Cette petite paysanne ignorante qui ne savait signer que d'une croix, tout de même en lettres de sang et d'or, elle a écrit un livre, et ce livre il était juste qu'elle fût la première à y porter les yeux» (*T,* II, 1514-15). We are told to listen to the rose, not just to smell it. Musique speaks of God's hand «qui écrit avec nous sur l'éternité en lignes courtes et longues, / Jusqu'aux virgules, jusqu'au point le plus imperceptible, / Ce livre qui n'aura son sens que quand il sera fini» (*T,* II, 789). The world itself is then a text which speaks to us. All creation is verbal: «Trop longtemps les romantiques nous ont fait croire que la création était muette, quand c'est eux qui n'écoutaient pas; alors que tout entière elle n'est que parole, langage, discours, drame, récit, argument, chant, musique» (*Opr,* 1396).

Man, we discover, is in search of the supreme word, the word which will express his essence. «O murmurant», cries Tête d'Or, «fais-moi part / De ce mot que je suis dont je sens en moi l'horrible effort!» (*T,* I, 182). Mesa also shares in these birth pangs: «Et soi-même, ceci seulement, eh quoi, / Que l'on est totalement clair, lisible, mais que l'on se sente actuellement / Prononcé / Comme un mot supporté par la voix et par l'intonation de son verbe! / O le tourment de se sentir épelé comme de quelqu'un qui n'en vient pas à bout! Il ne me laisse pas de repos!» (*T,* I, 1001). Finally, Pierre speaks of that unknown word which he feels growing within him (*T,* I, 574).

This is the essential word, more precious than a diamond, through which we will be united with God—the complete word, the word par excellence which is our root and key and which, in the plenitude of its meaning, is a partial image of God. This is the word which we will release when we die as a flower does its perfume. At this supreme instant we will express our true meaning, we will make restitution, we will return to God that word through which we were made. It is for this reason that the poet prays: «Mais que je trouve seulement la parole juste, que j'exhale seulement /

Cette parole de mon coeur, l'ayant trouvée, et que je meure ensuite, l'ayant dite» (*Opo,* 251).

And this word, which Christ came to teach us, is none other than *Father: Pater, pater noster, Abba*—the word through which we express our meaning and substance, our true identity as sons of God. At the time of death our soul is said to escape with this cry, a cry which can be likened to the cry of an infant entering into life. (And since this verbal explosion, this cry, reveals the essence of our very being, since it defines us, Claudel concludes: «L'âme dépouillé de son corps et de ce qui était autour d'elle opaque et immobile, / Ne peut être comparée qu'à un cri et à ce mouvement pur de la substance intelligente et affective» [*Opo,* 611].)

Considering then the significance of the word, we are not surprised to discover that of all our senses Claudel should feel that hearing is the most important. What is surprising, however, is the magnitude of this importance.

Our ears, we learn, are the organs most appropriate for communication with the invisible and since God is invisible, hearing is the faculty best suited for communication with Him. As Claudel says: «L'appareil auditif est par excellence l'organe de la Foi» (*Oc,* XX, 262). It is then through this faculty that we come into contact with God—the Word made flesh. And our union with Him at this level is far more perfect than at any other. The verbalization of the Deity makes an exchange possible. «Le Verbe de Dieu est Celui en qui Dieu s'est fait à l'homme donnable / La parole créée est cela en qui toutes choses créées sont faites à l'homme donnables» (*Opo,* 281). The assimilation on this plane exceeds even that afforded through Holy Communion. «Vous ne m'avez pas donné de pauvre à nourrir, ni de malade à panser, / Ni de pain à rompre, mais la parole qui est reçue plus complètement que le pain et l'eau, et l'âme soluble dans l'âme» (*Opo,* 283). (The theme of eating, now on a verbal level, also reappears in the following passage: «Et moi, pressé par le bruit intérieur, je voulais proposer au monde un mot soluble et délectable, / Afin de repaître comme un profond estomac la mémoire et l'intelligence comme une bouche bordée de lèvres avec ses dents» [*T*, I, 434]. In the same vein, the Viceroy speaks of words as having a delicious pulp [*T*, II, 765]. Claudel also refers to His blood as the eternal Word and adds that «la nourriture est une parole avalée» [*T*, I, 1309].) Union with God in this sphere can only be compared to that which might be attained through breathing. For God is like the air—He is heard and breathed. «Est-ce que tu sais qui est Dieu? Dis, est-ce que c'est comme le vent qu'on entend? On ne le voit pas, mais on est comme un aveugle qui entend, et c'est comme l'air» (*T*, I, 540).

In Claudel's universe, since all things are verbalized through Christ («Verbe en qui tout est parole») we often find that hearing replaces our other senses. In *L'Histoire de Tobie et de Sara,* for instance, Azarias speaks of lending an ear to Sara's perfume (*T*, II, 1297) and in *La Lune à la recherche d'elle-même* we learn that it is the poet's function to listen to his inner vision (*T*, II, 1321). Then in *Le Repos du septième jour* the Emperor's mother tells us that she is blind to the light which enters through the ears (*T*, I, 820) and the Emperor himself says: «Tous mes sens ne sont plus qu'un, et, confondu avec l'entendement, / Ceci est l'organe multiple de la contemplation dans l'extase» (*T*, I, 847). Finally, let us recall the title of Claudel's celebrated volume of art criticism: *L'Oeil écoute.*

Of all the senses vision is perhaps the one most often contrasted with hearing. Claudel says of the two: «La vue est l'organe de l'approbation active, de la conquête intellectuelle, tandis que l'ouïe est celui de la réceptivité» (*Opr,* 189). Vision is a masculine, aggressive faculty. It is the faculty through which we make contact with the outside world. «Connaître par conséquent, c'est nous informer, c'est naître, c'est nous constituer existants par rapport à cette chose là-bas qui de son côté est en train de pourvoir à sa propre existence, par le moyen de cet oeil actif qui etablit un contact» (*Oc,* XXII, 325). As a result, vision entails considerable violence. Ysé exclaims: «Ah! je les connais, il y a longtemps que je les attendais, ces yeux dévorants pour me regarder! et pour me faire du mal!» (*T*, I, 1192). Louis Laine remarks: «Je ne vois plus tes yeux. Tu ne me regardes pas. Je n'ai plus peur» (*T*, I, 761). And Prouhèze speaks of the devouring question in Camille's eyes (*T*, II, 833).

But then Mesa cries out: «Moi qui aimais tellement ces choses visibles, ô j'aurais voulu tout voir, avoir avec appropriation» (*T*, I, 1001) and we know that he is giving expression to some of Claudel's most intimate longings, the longings of Tête d'Or, the longings which Claudel like his heroes, is called upon to renounce. The feminine within him, his soul, his spirituality, his receptive faculties—all struggle for hegemony. It is so that this femininity might triumph that so many of Claudel's characters are blind or blinded. Violaine and Pensée naturally come to mind first, but there is also the blindfolded man in *La Sagesse ou la parabole du festin* who is led by a woman. There is Tobie who describes himself as «ce pauvre vieillard à qui Vous avez pris soin d'ôter la vue afin qu'il entende mieux» (*T*, II, 1280). The same thing is then done to his wife and for the same reasons. In a sense it is so that her vision might be perfected that her eyesight is removed. After having been blinded she cries: «Je vous entends! Il n'y a pas besoin d'yeux pour ça! l'ange m'a dit qu'à jamais je ne cesserai plus de vous voir! avec autre chose que mes yeux! avec mon coeur, avec mes oreilles!» (*T*, II, 1318). Similarly, the poet in *La Lune à la recherche d'elle-même* tells us that when he wants to see something he closes his eyes (*T*, II, 1331) and Beata in «Cantate à trois voix» exclaims: «Éteins cette lumière! / Éteins promptement cette lumière qui ne me permet de voir que ton visage!» (*Opo*, 372).

When Rodrigue speaks of «ces mots qu'elle ne sait pas qu'elle me dit, et je n'ai qu'à fermer les yeux pour les entendre» (*T*, II, 697), we again see that these two faculties —seeing and hearing—do not complement each other, but instead seem to be in conflict. That they represent two radically different modes of experience becomes apparent in the following remarks made by Musique: «Je veux le remplir tout à coup et le quitter instantanément, et je veux qu'il n'ait alors aucun moyen de me retrouver, et pas les yeux et les mains, mais le centre seul et ce sens en nous de l'ouïe qui s'ouvre» (*T*, II, 709). Seeing is concrete and physical. It is associated with hands and touching or grabbing. Hearing is ethereal and spiritual. As mentioned above, seeing is masculine in character; hearing is feminine. In this connection we note that many of Claudel's female characters boast of excellent hearing—Violaine and Pensée, of course, but Marthe also. She tells us: «J'écoute; peu de gens savent écouter» (*T*, I, 665). Lechy claims: «J'ai l'oreille fine comme une pie!» (*T*, I, 684). Even Mara makes a similar boast, saying to Jacques: «C'est vrai, tu n'entends rien. Mais moi, j'ai l'oreille vivante». But then she adds: «Et le jas de l'oeil ouvert» (*T*, II, 115) and this betrays deafness on a more profound level, a deafness which she admits to when she cries: «Mais moi, je suis sourde et je n'entends pas! et je crie vers toi de la profondeur où je suis!» (*T*, II, 77). Mesa makes a similar confession when he moans: «Je ne puis plus supporter d'être sourd et mort!» (*T*, I, 1052).

As we can see, this deafness is intimately connected with spiritual death which, interestingly enough, implies an inability to communicate orally, as is demonstrated in the following passage: «L'esprit obscur appelé Asmodée ... est muet, et il a de quoi s'entendre avec tout ce qui dans l'homme n'a pas appris à parler, etant sourd» (*T*, II, 1293). It is obviously an internal principle of verbal expression that Claudel associates with our spirituality: «Comme la vierge a fait le Christ il s'agit pour nous de le faire aussi. Il s'agit à long labeur de s'arranger de *ce principe en nous qui parle* et de lui fournir forme et visage, et instrument à son intention, afin qu'une fois de plus *le Verbe se fasse chair*» (*Oc*, XX, 177).

Hearing, then, is vital to the rebirth process. We learn in fact that there is an ear hidden in our inner being which is like a matrix or womb. We also discover that the voice is a creative force. It was God's voice that called us into existence. This was the case with Joan of Arc: «C'est une voix qui est venue éveiller l'âme de Jeanne et qui lui a appris à vibrer» (*T,* II, 1515). So it is also with us. The creative nature of this call is revealed when Ysé tells Mesa: «Il ... faut ... m'appeler ... par de tels mots ... qu'ils ne soient pas ailleurs que dans mon coeur, bien lourds comme l'enfant inconnu qu'on porte lorsque l'on est grosse» (*T,* I, 1023). Later she adds: «J'entends la voix dans mes entrailles comme une chose énorme et massive et aveugle et désirante et taciturne» (*T,* I, 1112). Finally she asks: «Donne-moi seulement l'accord, que jaillisse, / Comme une voix véritable à ta voix, ton éternelle Ysé» (*T,* I, 1139). Pensée says that it is as Orian speaks that she comes into existence (*T,* II, 545) and Rodrigue refers to the wounding capabilities of the voice when he begs: «Perce mon coeur avec cette voix inconnue, avec ce chant qui n'a jamais existé!» (*T,* II, 830). This, of course, is the wounding which is associated with the love experience and with new birth. (The power of the voice and its role in the love relationship is described as follows: «Puissance merveilleuse de la voix, de l'âme directement qui atteint, qui imprègne, qui s'unit l'autre âme et qui l'entraîne avec elle, avec la connivence irrésistible de l'oreille, dans un même acte d'amour, quand c'est l'amour qui va à la rencontre de la foi!» [*Oc,* XVI, 204]. In like manner, the voice is also said to be the expression of our union with God. «La voix qui est à la fois l'esprit et l'eau, l'élément plastique et la volonté qui s'impose à elle, est l'expression de cette union bienheureuse [entre nous et Dieu]» [*Opo,* 234].)

Claudel's most audacious statement concerning the creative function of the voice was made by Mara, however. «Et le Verbe s'est fait chair et il a habité parmi nous! / Et le cri de Mara, et l'appel de Mara, et le rugissement de Mara, et lui aussi, il s'est fait chair au sein de cette horreur, au sein de cette ennemie, au sein de cette personne en ruine, au sein de cette abominable lépreuse! / Et cet enfant qu'elle m'avait pris, / Du fond de mes entrailles j'ai crié si fort qu'à la fin

je le lui ai arraché, je l'ai arraché de cette tombe vivante»
(*T,* II, 124). And also: «Cette voix, cette même voix de
sa soeur qui un certain jour de Noël a fait force jusqu'au fond
de ses entrailles!» (*T,* II, 124). The voice, that aggressive,
masculine force, can also penetrate God's domain. «Ce qui
ouvre le mur de Dieu ce n'est point la lance, / Mais le cri
d'un coeur affligé, car le royaume de Dieu souffre violence»
(*Opo,* 432). It is said that the human voice is weaker than
the savage cry of animals, yet it reaches the skies and pierces
the envelope of the earth—the earth which is our flesh.

As we can see, the creativity described above reveals that
man is possessed of powers to give life and to call things
into existence—powers which mirror the divine prerogatives.
Claudel explains this by reminding us that we were all
created in His image, and since He is creative— the Creator—
so are we all. He has implanted in the innermost reaches
of our being a portion of His virtue, of His power to call
things and people into existence. Since He is the creative
Word, we are not surprised to discover that this power is
closely linked with verbal expression. That this is the case
in Claudel's universe has been amply demonstrated. So when
Mesa asks Ysé: «Est-ce que tu m'entends à présent? est-ce
que tu sens vivre / Mon souffle au fond de tes entrailles?
est-ce que tu es sous ma parole comme quelqu'un de créé?»
(*T,* I, 1053). We know what creative forces are at work.

But for Claudel there also exists a creativity which would
encompass the entire universe. This is the creativity of the
poet whose role was described in the beginning of this chapter
in the following terms: «C'est l'univers entier que nous
inhalons par la contemplation et par l'intelligence et que nous
restituons à Dieu après avoir fait du chant, du sens et de
l'esprit» (*Oc,* XXV, 539). Yet in Claudel the creative nature
of the poetic function would seem even to surpass this its
priestly aspect for just as it is said that God created each
being by naming him so it is said of the poet: «Quand tu
parles, ô poëte, dans une énumération délectable / Proférant
de chaque chose le nom, / Comme un père tu l'appelles

mystérieusement dans son principe, et selon que jadis / Tu participas à sa création, tu coopères, à son existence!» (*Opo*, 230). (How and why the poet participated in the original creation was explained in Chapter I, p. 17 and will be discussed again later.) It might even be claimed that in a certain mode he actually brings nature into existence: «Les yeux plus longtemps fermés qu'ouverts, l'artiste profère un mot. Le *mot* de l'enchanteur qui crée. Et la nature, comme si elle n'existait pas, *elle apparaît*» (*Opr*, 1517). (Despite appearances to the contrary, in this passage Claudel is referring to the art of the painter. It therefore should be remarked that pictoral production is included in the realm of verbal expression and that the role of vision is minimal even in this sphere. Both of these factors corroborate what was said above concerning the faculties of hearing and vision.) We also learn that the poet is able to impose his order on nature: «O poëte, je ne dirai point que tu reçois de la nature aucune leçon, c'est toi qui imposes ton ordre. / Toi, considérant toutes choses! / Pour voir ce qu'elle répondra tu t'amuses à appeler l'une après l'autre par son nom» (*Opo*, 230).

And the word he creates does not perish. We see that there exists something within the poet which is capable of transforming all that is transitory «en une lumière stable» (*Oc*, XXV, 442). This internal principle inhales what is temporal and changes it into eternity. It is a principle with which the poet would be entirely identified. «Et moi qui fais les choses éternelles avec ma voix, faites que je sois tout entier / Cette voix, une parole totalement intelligible!» (*Opo*, 243).

Now that we know the scope of the artist's power, let us turn our attention to the actual production of the word, a fascinating operation which begins with a kind of «ivresse», «spasme mortel», or explosion that might be likened to the sexual orgasm. It is described as follows: «Soudain le coup sourd au coeur, soudain le mot donné, soudain le souffle de l'Esprit, le rapt sec, soudain la possession de l'Esprit!» (*Opo*, 234). A fitting prelude indeed to a process that can only be compared with childbirth. «Voici soudain, quand le poëte nouveau comblé de l'explosion intelligible, / La clameur noire de toute la vie nouée par le nombril dans la commotion de la base, / S'ouvre, l'accès / Faisant sauter la clôture, le souffle de lui-même / Violentant les mâchoires coupantes, / Le frémissant Novénaire avec un cri!» (*Opo,* 222). In keeping with this description, Pierre in *La Jeune Fille Violaine* speaks of the birth of the word in these terms: «La parole ... se forme ... longuement, obscurément, / Plus profond que le coeur et les intestins, ... elle se constitue, / Comme un oeuf spirituel en nous, comme la capsule seminale, / Jusqu'à ce que du lien qui la lie se dissolve le secret pédoncle» (*T,* I, 573). We also hear Avare say: «Mais en moi, comme la femme qui dans son coeur éprouve la commotion de l'enfant mâle, vit / La parole qui a l'oreille pour langue, et cela, comme un captif, / Avec propriété réclame l'action et la liberté» (*T,* I, 453). Finally, Claudel describes his poetic mission as follows: «J'ai une chose à dire et il faut absolument que je la dise; Dieu ... l'a mise en moi afin que je la produise dans le travail et la douleur» (*T,* I, 1294). (This latter phrase naturally brings to mind the divine curse pronounced against woman in Genesis—that she give birth in pain and suffering.)

We must not assume, however, that the poet's creative function stops here, for the poet is also a «semeur» by vocation, as we can see from the following prayer: «Faites que je sois un semeur de solitude et que celui qui entend ma parole / Rentre chez lui inquiet et lourd» (*Opo,* 283). Once the poet is delivered of the word it must be implanted in the human heart like pollen in a flower. There it will germinate and grow. So just as we have learned that the divine word will not return to God empty and sterile, we now discover that the same is true of the poet's word. «Le Verbe est créateur, tout mot à qui les lèvres de l'homme procurent existence évoque, toute vérité qu'il exprime provoque en vastes zones concentriques une séries d'échos, de réponses, de souvenirs d'appels, de contradictions, une espèce de chant ou de champs autour d'elle corollaire, une modification de la circonstance par l'idée, l'ébranlement de l'âme par le son, l'accueil fait par les délegués au moment de la nature et de la durée à une proposition temporelle» (*T*, II, 1504). The word once proffered has a life of its own, a certain internal dynamism. It is like a seed which attracts to itself all the elements necessary for its own realization, for its own development. The poet in addition to being creator of the word is also sower of the word. Here again we see that he duplicates the divine prerogatives, for it is said that God became a seed in the Virgin's breast and that His mission with us is that of sower.

It now appears appropriate to discuss woman's role in all of this, for it would seem that the poet has usurped the creative function, a function which in Chapters I and II we declared to be distinctly feminine. We might well ask at this point if the age-old masculine desire to preempt or at least emulate woman's creativity has here been realized. Time and again an effort is made in this direction by Claudel and his virile heroes. Pierre is said to give birth to his churches. Avare, as we have seen, is the mother of his word, like Claudel. Even Tête d'Or speaks of himself as «[une] mère meilleure».

If we search for an outside opinion on this matter, we hear it said: «The creative process has a feminine quality, and the created work arises from unconscious depths—we might truly say from the realm of the Mothers» (1). Again: «Man produces his work as a complete creation out of his inner feminine self» (2). It is only because man has an underlying feminine principle that he is able to create—and when we recall Claudel's theories on the bisexuality of man we realize that, despite appearances to the contrary, he himself was aware of this reality, painfully so. As we are reminded: «Ce n'est pas avec le tour et le ciseau que l'on fait un homme

---

(1) Carl G. Jung, *The Spirit in Man, Art, and Literature,* trans. by R. F. C. Hull, Bollingen Series XX (New York City: Pantheon Books, 1966), p. 103.
(2) Jung, *Two Essays,* p. 230.

vivant, mais avec une femme, ce n'est pas avec l'encre et la plume que l'on fait une parole vivante! / Quel compte donc fais-tu des femmes? tout serait trop facile sans elles» (*Opo,* 268).

There is ample proof of the importance of the feminine principle in this sphere. Claudel admits, for instance, that as a poet he isn't «un fabricant». He believes in inspiration —an inspiration of which he is not master, which chooses its own moment to appear. An inspiration from which he receives the creative impetus—a seed, an enigmatic and form-less word. An inspiration which, as we might well suppose, comes from none other than the feminine principle within, Anima or the poet's muse (who is at times associated with Grace or Sophia). It is only through contact with her that the poet is made fertile and is able to deliver the word. His role in this operation is merely to keep himself open and attentive. It is only through and because of her that the poet can claim that he was present at creation, that he participates in creation, or that his words are eternal. For, as pointed out in Chapter I, Anima is identified with Sophia, God's creative wisdom. It is through her that man is anterior to death and it is in her that man touches the divine, that he is divine, that he will be united with the divine. «O part! ô réservée! ô partie antérieure de moi-même qui étais avant moi! / O partie de moi-même qui es étrangère à tout lieu et ma ressemblance éternelle qui / Touches à certains nuits / Mon coeur» (*Opo,* 273).

She imparts the word, but then again she also is the word. Sara remarks: «Je suis cette parole en pleine figure de la vie!» (*T,* II, 1297) and Camille speaks of that word from God which Prouhèze is for Rodrigue (*T,* II, 1086). Then in *La Sagesse ou la parabole du festin* we see Wisdom clad in writing and in *La Ville, deuxième version* we hear Ivors speak of the mystery of Sophia which he associates with the divine language of poetry (*T,* I, 476). (We also recall that the Word is compared to an eternal young girl in «L'Esprit et l'eau».) But it is only when Claudel asks the following question that we know he has fully identified Anima with the word: «Où est-il, ce mot essentiel enfin, plus précieux que le diamant, / Cette goutte d'eau pour qu'elle se fonde en Vous, notre âme, comme l'amante en son amant?» (*Opo,* 494). We can now conclude that this word, this seed of God within us, this part of us which will be united with Him is beyond any shadow of a doubt feminine.

Anima's roles in Claudel's verbal universe are many and varied. Not only is she the word, but she is also the very breath which supports that word, as Sara reveals: «Je suis cette haleine impérissable à qui l'a une fois respirée!» (*T,* II, 1297). Like woman in the love relationship, it is she who poses the question which initiates the poetic relationship, a question the importance of which can be determined from the following remarks: «Je suis un homme qui répond à une question. Un homme qui toute sa vie n'a jamais fait autre chose que de prêter l'oreille à une question. La même question. La question urgente, intense, tenace.... Une question et c'était la réponse seule, je le sais, qui me permettait d'y comprendre quelque chose. Quelle exigence!» (*T,* II, 1402). But then we also hear him say, and this to his muse: «Je lis une réponse, je lis une question dans tes yeux! Une réponse et une question dans tes yeux!» (*Opo,* 233) and we discover that the answer lies in her just as the question emanated from her. As might be expected, however, this answer is not easy to discern. The muse explains: «Et je ne te laisserai point aller du pas des autres bonhommes ta route, / Jusque tu aies tout deviné cela que je veux dire, et celle-là n'est pas facile à entendre / Qui n'a point voix ni bouche» (*Opo,* 272).

But Anima has other functions. She is said to give man creative sleep. The importance of this becomes apparent when we realize that it is in this state that man is most productive, as was the case with Adam, for here he comes into contact with his unconscious, his soul. It is for this reason that Coeuvre calls Lala «Sommeil obscur». She is his inspiration and he says of her: «Tes mains ... donnent le sommeil. / Car il faut que je dorme afin que tu attouches mon âme et que tu reçoives / Mon souffle et que j'ai avec toi communication» (*T*, I, 446). The role of sleep in the creative process is further clarified by Pierre, from whom we learn: «Et c'est ainsi que souvent le sommeil, d'une pression aveugle, / Délivre la pensée en nous formée au-dessous de notre connaissance» (*T*, I, 573). This is the aforementioned «realm of the Mothers».

Anima is also said to be responsible for the overwhelming ambitions of the poet. She prods him and requires that his scope encompass all of creation. «Qu'exiges-tu de moi? est-ce qu'il me faut créer le monde pour le comprendre? Est-ce qu'il me faut engendrer le monde et le faire sortir de mes entrailles? / O oeuvre de moi-même dans la douleur! ô oeuvre de ce monde à te représenter!» (*Opo*, 274). With this lament we begin to understand some of the poet's misgivings regarding his muse. It is in fact interesting to examine the relationship between the two, a relationship which will of course mirror the one described in Chapter II between Claudel's men and women who represent the poet's inner multiplicity.

Claudel has said that inspiration is inimitable and that no measure of talent or artifice could possibly replace it. Yet he also warns of its dangers, dangers which some poets have underestimated—Rimbaud, for instance, or Hugo whom Claudel characterizes as «un incontestable Inspiré qui ne se méfiait pas assez de l'inspiration» (*Opr*, 474). Claudel tells of the suspicious elements which can accompany inspiration and which justify prudence. It is a phenomenon which is both inestimable and dangerous. This ambiguity is explained to some extent in the following passage: «Dans toute figure de femme il y a ça. Il y a Anima. Il y a la Grâce, tout ce qui est un élément qui échappe au raisonnement, qui est imprévu, qui est la fantaisie ... qui peut aussi bien avoir un sens mauvais qu'un bon sens. Cette femme qui est la Grâce peut devenir aussi la femme qui est la perdition mais elle ne perd pas pour ça le même caractère de l'une et la contre-partie de l'autre» (*Mi*, 93). The duality which permeates all of Claudel's works has made another appearance. Here we encounter once again the Claudelian syzygy discussed in Chapter II which corresponds to both external and internal reality, to both woman and the soul. Standing next to «la Muse qui est la Grâce», or to be replaced by her, is the earthly muse whom Claudel calls «mon antique soeur des ténèbres».

For the poet the most disturbing attribute of his muse is undoubtedly her independence. As she says: «Je ne suis pas accesible à la raison, tu ne feras point, tu ne feras point de moi ce que tu veux, mais je chante et je danse!» (*Opo*, 268). Man will never succeed in dominating his dreams, his inspiration or his soul. With reason we hear him complain: «Mais toi, je n'ai aucun droit sur toi et qui peut savoir quand tu viens?» (*Opo*, 273). Even his contact with the muse who is Grace is humiliating for she informs him that it was not he who chose her but rather she who chose him and this even before he was born. Also disturbing is the fact that the woman within would lead man where he fears to go. She would have him abandon reason and duty. The poet resists, crying out: «J'ai durement acquis d'etre homme» (*Opo*, 270), a remark which betrays the intensity of his inner struggle.

It is perhaps because of the violence and danger implicit in this relationship that the soul is so often called a sword. (Lumîr says: «Il y a moyen de sortir l'âme du corps comme une épée» [*T*, II, 474]. Mesa calls Ysé «l'âme outrée, sortie de ton corps comme une épée à demi dégainée» [*T*, I, 1137]. And, finally, Claudel commands: «Dégage-toi de cette chair molle! dégaine, comme une épée ton âme, cette armature intérieure» [*T*, II, 1535].) But this violence and danger also take on other guises. In «Judith», the heroine, who represents Wisdom or the soul, wields a lethal sword with which she slays Holopherne, a deed which obviously symbolizes the necessary, but dreaded, killing of the old man which must preceed rebirth. There is also violence and cruelty implicit in the so-called infidelity of the soul—that faithless wife—which is described as follows: «Cette note secrète, cette syllabe sacrée, que nous essayons de défendre au fond de nous jusqu'à ce que le mystérieux ravisseur ait trouvé pour la séduire et l'entraîner avec lui la proposition irrésistible!» (*Opr,* 361). Claudel speaks of God as having stolen his soul and like a jealous lover he complains: «Ce n'est pas à moi que s'adressent cette figure rayonnante et ces yeux qui ne sont plus de la terre et ces lèvres cruelles toutes frémissantes déjà d'un aveu que bientôt je serai impuissant à retenir! [Elle] ne veut plus revenir avec moi» (*Oc,* V, 241).

As we have seen in Chapter II, woman in Claudel's universe mirrors all of these characteristics. Her relationship with man is fraught with violence, frustration, and misgivings. She is capricious, fanciful, earthy, and cruel. Given a chance, she would dominate man and lead him into that death which he so greatly fears. Yet she is also grace, light, and music. And she has it in her power to impart that life which he also greatly fears. We are left to conclude that she is so because she is a creature of the poet's imagination and as such an image of Anima.

Let us now complete our discussion of this subject by examining yet another theme. Let us briefly explore the role of music in Claudel's verbal universe.

The poet tells us that his poetic doctrine could be summed up in the words of Sophia: «*N'empêchez pas la musique. Laissez-la émaner toute seule. Arrangez-vous pour qu'elle émane*» (*Opr,* 55). We are to act in such a way that our actions and even our most secret thoughts do not disrupt the harmony of which we are a part. We are instead to foster that harmony, to create it around us. For Claudel this maxim, «N'empêchez pas la musique», encompasses all morality. It exhorts us to act on two levels. First, it would have us do nothing which would obliterate the delicate awareness of our personal melody line. This is an awareness which permits us to find our way among the diversity of exterior propositions. It implies docility to our feminine souls from which this personal melody line emanates, as we shall see.

Secondly, it would have us develop our spiritual lives through prayer and watchfulness.

In this realm Claudel is in full agreement with St. Augustine who said that the world was a melody and that history was like the modulation of an immense musical phrase. The poet readily adopts this vision of world order but to it he adds the idea of respiratory rhythm, the rhythm of reciprocity and song. For Claudel the importance of music is such that the Emperor in *Le Repos du septième jour* is exhorted to govern according to its principles He is to maintain the eternal harmony between the visible and the invisible «écoutant d'une oreille et de l'autre / Afin qu'aucune note ne se fausse» (*T*, I, 857).

On another level Claudel tells us that all art is in rapport with music. He also speaks of an obscure musical invitation to unite all horizons, to unite all of creation. He associates music with our secret name and with our vocation. He tells us that it is an irresistible force. And we learn, as might have been suspected, that it is Sophia, whom we identified with song and dance in Chapter I, that will make us servants of music—Sophia, who is represented in man's feminine soul.

Woman or the feminine principle is consistently associated with music in Claudel's universe. It is said of the muse, for instance: «Tu n'es pas celle qui chante, tu es le chant même dans le moment qu'il s'élabore» (*Opo*, 226). Then we know that most of Claudel's heroines are musical. There is Musique, of course, but also the Princess who sings and dances, Lala who plays the violin and Sichel who is a pianist. Even Thalie and Jobarbara dance. We also know that Pensée's voice is like music to Orian. And Rodrigue says the same of Prouhèze's words.

But woman has even greater powers. Not only is she in harmony with the music of the spheres, a music which is divine in origin, but she also has the ability of causing others to enter into this state of harmony. Through her others begin to participate in the celestial melody. Musique says: «Mon chant est celui que je fais naître» (*T*, II, 764) and Orian notes: «Tout cela qu'il y avait en moi et que je ne connaissais pas, à mesure qu'elle parlait, tout cela ... fournissait en moi comme de la musique!» (*T*, II, 529). (Only the poet shares in this power, a power which he derives, however, from the feminine principle within.) It cannot be doubted that this music is celestial when we hear the following remark: «Saint-Père, qu'est-ce qu'il fait, celui qui n'a plus de péchés? Il Chante!» (*T*, II, 527). In fact the song within is not a product of our own active effort to compose it but rather the product of our passive ability to receive it. «Ce n'est pas moi qui chante, ce sont mes oreilles tout à coup qui se sont ouvertes! / Et qui sait si demain je ne serai pas redevenu sourd?» (*T*, II, 764). Here again we see the importance of hearing and we understand why woman in her passivity is more perceptive and therefore more in harmony with creation than her male counterpart.

Finally it should be remarked that in order to hear this melody, which is called the word of Sophia, we must create a stillness within. It is only when Animus keeps silent, when he surrenders to Anima, that she can express herself.

Through this silence, we will perceive, we will hear, we will come into contact with the silence which is the supreme expression of music and the word. As Michel Plourde observes, in Claudel's universe «la parole devient authentique pour autant qu'elle s'éloigne du son» (3). For this reason the poet prays: «Faites que je sois entre les hommes comme une personne sans visage et ma / Parole sur eux sans aucun son comme un semeur de silence» (*Opo,* 283). We have now left the aggressive realm of the spoken word and entered into the more spiritual sphere of silence, the sphere of «la parole qui a l'oreille pour langue» (*T*, I, 453). We realize that ultimate form of expression also exists for music when we recall how the Viceroy told Musique that she

---

(3) Michel Plourde, *Paul Claudel: Une Musique du silence* (Montréal: Les Presses de l'Université de Montréal, 1970), p. 359.

needed no strings for her guitar, or when we bring to mind the Satyre-Major's remark in *Protée:* «S'il s'agissait de faire du bruit, nous n'aurions pas besoin de musique. C'est le silence qu'il s'agit de faire entendre». Then we are told: «L'orchestre joue à vide, les violons retournés, les cymbales disjointes, les cuivres bouchés» (*T,* II, 333). Finally we hear it said: «Car si l'on peut contrarier la musique quand elle se fait entendre, comment lui résister quand elle se tait» (*Oc,* XX, 35).

The importance of this silence which Claudel calls «[un] silence qui est à la mesure de l'Éternite ... Non pas un silence vide, mais un silence comble, un silence chargé» (*Oc,* XXV, 505) undoubtedly stems from the fact that it is the supreme form of divine expression. «Taisez-vous seulement, / Mon Dieu», cries Mesa, «afin que votre créature entende! Qui a goûté à votre silence, / Il n'a pas besoin d'explication» (*T,* I, 1050). The silence of God then explains the silence of Mnemosyne. She never speaks because she is that part of the soul which is in contact with the Deity. In a similar manner her daughters, the other muses, are also silent. As Plourde tells us: «Elles ne parlent pas, mais elles poussent sur ce rythme crée, qui est désormais sorti du silence» (4). It is this rhythm, this «mesure sacrée», to which the poet must be attentive.

---

(4) Ibid., p. 358.

CHAPTER V

THE STRUGGLE FOR UNITY

In a brilliant article contained in his book *Le Livre à venir* Maurice Blanchot makes the following observation concerning Claudel: «Ce qui frappe en lui, c'est une discordance essentielle, le heurt puissant, contenu, mal contenu, de mouvements sans harmonie, un mélange formidable de besoins contraires, d'exigences opposées, de qualités désappareillées et d'aptitudes inconciliables» (1). He then goes on to illustrate this by giving us concrete examples. He points out how Claudel is both impetuous and slow. He is lacking in patience and yet obstinate, as abrupt as he is prudent, without method yet orderly, without measure though he finds the unbounded intolerable. He is a man of crises, both religious and amorous, but it takes him years to integrate his crucial experiences. As a poet he relies on inspiration, yet he composes with the regularity and assurance of a bureaucrat. Robert Mallet adds to this picture when he says: «Paul Claudel a de la carrure. Il se carre dans son fauteuil. Il vous attend au tournant de la conversation. Il sait, d'un rire ou d'un regard, vous remettre en selle. Que de rondeurs chez cet homme carré!» (2).

---

(1) Maurice Blanchot, *Le Livre à venir*, 4th ed. (Paris: Gallimard, 1959), p. 85.
(2) Stanislas Fumet, *Claudel*, 6th ed. (Paris: Gallimard, 1958), p. 10.

But these divisions and contradictions go still deeper. We might even venture to say that they originated at his birth, for as André Vachon points out, «les origines de Claudel, de quelque point de vue qu'on les considère, finissent toujours par présenter deux faces bien distinctes. Bourgeois et Vosgien par son père, le poète se rattache pourtant, par sa mère, à la paysannerie champenoise. Sur un tout autre plan, à l'esprit voltairien et libre-penseur du père, s'oppose le christianisme traditionnel de la mère» (3). Claudel alludes to this double heredity and its result when he says: «Beaucoup d'entre nous sentent dans leur intelligence et dans leur sang le conflit de cette double hérédité. Turelure et Coûfontaine vivent dans le même coeur» (T, II, 1425).

We also know that in Claudel's early adolescence his family moved to Paris at the insistence of Camille. This relocation occasioned a painful split in the household, for the poet's father was forced to remain in Vassy. Claudel tells us that this turn of events was catastrophic for him—as a result of it his whole life was torn in two. In Paris he suffered from what he calls «la solitude la plus absolue». He had nothing, no one from whom he could seek counsel.

Later, we see the same pattern emerge in Claudel's diplomatic career which required a great deal of travel. We hear him say that the two great desires of his life were to leave his country and to return. He tells us: «Je suis à la fois un voyageur et un enraciné» (Mi, 12). He also says: «Le Far-West et l'Extrême-Orient, ma vie a été partagée entre ces deux extrêmes» (J, II, 769). Finally, there is the fact that his life was divided between diplomacy and art.

Without a doubt, however, the greatest source of conflict for Claudel was his religion, for Christianity is a creed which seems to bring internal and external division to the believer. It is in fact a religion which in itself seems contradictory in

---

(3) Vachon, Le Temps, p. 33.

that it calls for both joy and suffering, love and renunciation, life through death.

After Claudel's conversion a new and formidable being came into existence, and this new being made terrible demands on the young poet. Claudel's aggressive instincts, his love of conquest, his passion for the earth, his attachment to the visible and concrete—all was now challenged by a religion which requires surrender and by a God who is invisible. (We are reminded of the conflict between seeing and hearing in Claudel's works. We recall that many of his heroes and heroines are blinded and for what reason.) On one side we have the conquering spirit of the young anarchist with his thirst for life and independence and on the other the conservative forces of conscience, family, and Church coupled with a hidden longing for security and protection. The past and the future battle within the young man's breast.

So we hear Claudel speak of the violent and painful contradiction which Christianity brought to all his instincts, a contradiction which he proposed to resolve through the evangelization of all his faculties. He speaks of preferring God to his body through a struggle waged against sensuality and of preferring God to his soul through a struggle waged against pride. He advocates spiritual opposition to bestial carnality, but then on the other hand he also recognizes the role of the flesh in deflating spiritual pride.

Claudel is a man at war with himself, but rightly so, for he proclaims that this battle is our most profound duty. In keeping with this Agnes Meyer describes Claudel as a bringer of strife. She says nothing is at peace in him. She speaks of the cleft which exists between his body and soul and of his need to fuse his passionate humanity with his no less great spiritual forces. She is of the opinion that it was his body which would not let him become a priest and that his soul feared life (4).

_____

(4) Meyer, «Note-Book», p. 163-64.

Claudel himself refers to this state of affairs when he says: «Comment concilier ces deux ordres de vérités superposés, et en apparence du moins étrangers l'un à l'autre, sinon contradictoires?   D'une part le monde de la réalité sensible ... celui aussi des désirs et des passions, et cet autre hors de lui si puissant, et si poignant ... Ce problème ... a été la cause en moi de tant de luttes intérieures et de tant de souffrances» (*Oc,* XX, 427).   We know of his initial solution to this problem: «Les parties ... de sensibilité, le besoin d'affection, etc. ... J'avais en somme, plus ou moins consciemment, à les refouler au profit de la formation rationnelle et spirituelle que je poursuivais» (*Mi,* 146).   But then he met Ysé.   Still no resolution was forthcoming—now, in fact, the cleft within becomes deeper.

Passing to the artistic realm, we might say that the poet's conversion was also a source of division in this sphere. (To demonstrate this we need only recall the conflict which developed in Claudel at this time between faith and imagination —imagination, that fearful vehicle of the unknown which Claudel links with concupiscence and the more suspect products of inspiration.)   But here the division proves fruitful. Now we begin to see some of the beneficial results of the aforementioned conflicts.   We discover that although Christianity is indeed a principle of contradiction, contradiction and opposition are necessary to art.   They alone provide the means of composition.   Claudel says: «Sans opposition, pas de composition» (*T,* II, 1474).   And then: «Le conflit essentiel que le christianisme anime en nous est le grand ressort dramatique» (*T,* II, 1411).   It is to this conflict that Claudel refers when he speaks of his feelings on finishing *Le Soulier de satin:* «Je sentais qu'en effet une grande partie de mon oeuvre était terminée, je sentais que le côté dramatique essentiel qui était en moi, ce que vous appelez le «mot», ce mot qui en réalité est un dialogue, avait épuisé l'effort de débat, de conflit qu'il pouvait y avoir en moi» (*Mi,* 306).   This dialogue obviously points to the existence of an internal reality consisting of two opposing forces which the poet personifies in his plays. These are the two forces which are implied when Claudel speaks of the human psyche as a house with two inhabitants—one lives on the main floor, the other in the basement. Each is in conflict with the other.

(In passing, let us remark the frequency with which this image of the house appears in Claudel's works. We read of «La Chambre intérieure», and of interior doors and windows. In *L'Échange* Lechy likens her soul to an empty house, Marthe is called «demeure de paix», and the burning mansion is linked with a human being gone mad. In *Le Soulier de satin* Pélage is identified with his house and he in turn speaks of the soul as being a palace hidden in the fog. Finally, we learn: «Tout au fond de l'escargot vide, / Se trouve un palais splendide, / Orné d'un miroir si petit / Que, pour y voir comme on est mis, / Il faut être une fourmi» [*Opo,* 977].)

More often than not these two internal boarders are characterized as being of opposite sexes. (Even in the two-floor house mentioned above, the basement tenant is said to be «craintivement choyé comme une maîtresse qu'on fait sortir à certaines heures de son harem occulte» [*T,* II, 1416] which partially establishes a feminine identity for this partner.) They are representatives of the yin and the yang, Anima and Animus, or the oft-mentioned left and right of the poet's inner being—Nada and Aliki in *Le Jet de pierre,* «la main gauche à la conquête de la main droite!» (*T,* II, 1248). Claudel says: «Descartes a dit ... qu'il faut diviser pour comprendre. Et soi-même, pourquoi pas? ... introduire le dialogue et la controverse entre la gauche et la droite de son esprit» (*Oc,* XXIII, 300). And as we have seen, it is from this dialogue that Claudel's theatre emerges.

Claudel tells us time and time again that most of his theatrical production represents an effort to shed light on his interior drama, that most of his characters represent different aspects of himself. For him one of the prime purposes of art is the purge of the soul. He speaks of deliverance through creation and of the violent struggle which filled the first twenty years of his literary life—the struggle for complete mastery over himself. It was not until he wrote *L'Otage,* in 1910, that he felt he had succeeded in creating objective, exterior characters for the first time. But is even this really true? Despite the poet's claims, we are forced to conclude that it is not, for we know how strongly Claudel identifies with the characters from the trilogy—with Orian who had wanted to be a priest, with Louis the parricide, and with Toussaint Turelure, for instance. As late as 1950 we hear him say that he still feels the blood of Toussaint Turelure boiling in his veins. Nor was *Le Soulier de satin,* written after 1910, what might be called an exterior play. Claudel admits instead that it was an explanation or a kind of realization of his interior world, of the movements of his soul and his thoughts. Even the characters in *Partage de midi,* who one would naturally assume to be exterior, may be demonstrated to be portraits of the poet's inner multiplicity. We need only recall the fact that *Fragment d'un drame* written twelve years prior to the poet's encounter with Rosalie L. is, by his own admission, a kind of first version of *Partage de midi.* (See Chapter II.)

As we can see, this creative phenomenon—the drama—has its source then in the depths of our being, in the unconscious, the realm of the Mothers. Claudel recognizes as much when he remarks: «Qui dira jusqu'à quelle profondeur dans le subconscient s'enfoncent les racines d'une oeuvre d'art?» (*T,* II, 1453). Even the theatre itself, that outer concrete reality, is referred to as «cette caverne abstraite et close» (*T,* II, 1472) or as «une cavité soustraite à notre espace, à notre temps practicables» (*T,* II, 1505). It is a womb and as such it corresponds in structure to the poet's inner psychic reality. Here the play comes into existence. Here it takes shape—a shape, however, which we soon discover the poet has little to do in determining.

Claudel's characters are independent. They often develop and act in ways which surprise and even disturb the poet. They follow their own logic. Claudel has this to say concerning the characters in *L'Annonce faite à Marie,* for instance: «Moi, je n'avais réussi qu'à peupler le sous-sol de ma conscience d'une poignée de locataires mécontents qui ne me laissèrent pas de repos ... pendant bien des années, sans jamais me laisser complètement ignorant de leurs sourdes intrigues et privé de leurs communications diurnes et nocturnes, ils trafiquèrent je ne sais quoi sous la présidence d'un nouveau venu appelé Pierre de Craon. Jusqu'à ce qu'arrivât, bien inattendu, le moment d'irruption!» (*T,* II, 1394). Elsewhere he adds: «Il est curieux que dans le travail littéraire on ne fait pas du tout ce qu'on veut, mais qu'on soit amené là où on ne voulait pas aller; oui, un artiste n'est pas absolument libre» (5). J. P. Kempf and J. Petit point out how this was the case with *L'Otage.* «Il est vrai, toutefois, que le poète avait voulu faire de ce drame historique, aux personnages symboliques, le drame du sacrifice, et que, d'une certaine manière, les personnages lui ont échappé» (6). Our critics point to the ambiguity of the ending to prove their contention. Sygne refuses to complete her sacrifice. The reader or viewer can only suppose what this refusal implies. «Cette obscurité du dénouement est très importante. Claudel ne l'a pas voulue, il l'a subie, ou plutôt découverte, à mesure que ses personnages prenaient vie; elle s'est imposée à lui» (7).

Claudel furnishes an explanation for all of these mysterious occurrences: «Avec le drame nous pénétrons dans la région la plus obscure du cerveau humain, celle du rêve. Dans le rêve, notre esprit, réduit à un état passif ou semi-passif, celui de *plateau,* est envahi par des fantômes—d'où venus? Pas seulement de la mémoire—qui séduisent notre collaboration à la perpétration d'un évènement. Eh bien, j'appellerai le drame un rêve dirigé» (*Opr,* 52-53). Then, concerning these *fantômes,* he states in another very important passage: «P.

---

(5) Jean-Pierre Kempf and Jacques Petit, «*L'Otage*», *Archives des Lettres Modernes,* No. 69 (1966), 51-52.
(6) Ibid., p. 49.
(7) Ibid., p. 53.

C. ... n'est pas seul, il a emmené avec lui toute une procession transparente, le quatuor vocal, la tribu intérieure, tous ces gens en nous faits d'une voix, d'un nom et d'un bout de visage, tout ce dialogue en nous femelle et mâle, tous ces dépouillés à la recherche de leur peau, toutes ces ombres afin d'être qui profitent de notre cavité!» (*Oc,* V, 247). With this we get a better picture of his dream world. It is peopled with a multitude of inhabitants—a multiplicity which reduces itself quite naturally, however, to simpler terms. Claudel mentioned, for instance, the basic dichotomy between that which is masculine and that which is feminine within—the right and left of his psyche. But then he also introduced a new element, the importance of which I would now like to discuss.

This new element is the «quatuor». With it we discover that the poet's inner dialogue somehow naturally divides itself among four interlocutors. His inner diversity is portrayed by four main protagonists who carry on the basic male-female exchange. That Claudel felt this four-part structure to be a natural one for psychic products becomes obvious in the following passage: «Supposons ce musicien qui a souffert de l'Amérique, qui par ailleurs a réussi à en mieux connaître les différents ingrédients, les différents éléments qui occasionnent cette souffrance, ce musicien sera en possession de quatre thèmes qu'il fera composer dans les mouvements de son inspiration» (*Mi,* 129-30).

Before beginning our discussion of the theme of the *quatuor,* let us first consider if it was of any conscious importance to the poet. Could Claudel have intended that numbers have any significance in his work?

We find our answer in the following remarks: «J'aurais encore beaucoup de choses à te dire sur la valeur symbolique de ce qu'on appelle d'un terme bien profond *les opérations arithmétiques,* comme s'il y avait dans un nombre une sorte de vertu essentielle infuse et d'activité essentielle» (*Oc,* XXVI, 78). Then: «Les chiffres peuvent changer, mais leurs rapports sont invariables et éternels. / Qui entend la géometrie n'aura point de déception dans le Ciel» (*Opo,* 623). In keeping with this we also hear him speak of «l'éternelle région des Nombres, la région des choses qui ne cessent pas» (*T,* II, 119).

So we see that there need be no equivocation on our part in this matter. Numbers were indeed significant to Claudel, and in his works we notice that the number four seems to carry special weight. It even rivals the number three in importance and three, as we know, is the preeminent number in Christian thought. But the number four also appears frequently in orthodox symbolism and this factor seems to have influenced the poet. Claudel often cites the four rivers of paradise, the four wounds of Christ, the four creatures of the Apocalypse, the four creatures with four faces in Ezekiel's vision, the four cardinal virtues, the four banners under which the Jews were said to have marched into the promised land, the four evangelists with their symbols, and the four Gospels. He also remarks that the number four recalls the Tetragrammaton or four letters forming the mystical name of the Creator. These are the four cardinal points of the Word, indeed of all language.

As one might suspect, the poet also associates the number four with the square. (Three naturally suggests the triangle.) The square is «cette raison centrale et fondamentale de tous côtés égale et parallèle à elle-même, qui est le siège du Verbe. Car Il est assis sur le carré, sur la pierre angulaire et sur l'entrecroisement du quadruple Évangile. C'est là-dessus qu'éternellement la messe est dite» (*Oc,* XIX, 314). (This is all mirrored, on a pagan level, in both *Tête d'Or* and *Le Repos du septième jour.* In *Tête d'or* the hero's wounded body is placed on a square rock which had once been used for ancient rites and in *Le Repos du septième jour* mention is made of a magic square and we are told that the Emperor sits on a square throne.)

On another plane Claudels tells us that the number three is like the soul and the number four like the body. It might also be said that the number three pertains to the Deity whereas four is the figure of humanity. Three represents divine virtue and four the creation. The human heart, although shaped like a triangle, has four compartments. The human body has four limbs. There are four seasons. The earth is composed of four elements and it is also said to have four horizons, four beaches, or four cardinal points—a fact which is most significant, for according to Claudel these four exterior points of orientation have their interior, psychological counterparts. He tells us, for instance, that «le quatuor de *L'Échange* représentait quatre aspects de la même personne, si vous voulez, comme ces statues que j'ai vues à Angkor: une idole qui a quatre visages, tournés vers les quatre points cardinaux» (*Mi,* 221).

The significance of this four-fold internal structure becomes apparent in the following:

> «*La cité était posée en carré.*» Que faut-il entendre par là? C'est l'image des camps romains ou des villes chinoises qui se présentent d'abord à notre esprit. Et nous nous reportons aussi à ce répertoire symbolique de l'Humanité, qui applique partout à la Terre, comme aux champs cultivés qui la subdivisent, entre ses quatre horizons la figure du carré. L'homme ne se sent chez lui, il ne se sent capable de faire acte de propriété, qu'au milieu de cette limitation inexpugnable de quatre parallèles qu'il accentue et consacre par des fosses, par des murs et par le bornage cadastral. Le carré, établi sur l'intersection du plan polaire nord-sud avec le cours du soleil et des planètes est l'ouest, est pour lui la cellule sociale comme l'hexagone l'est pour les abeilles. Maintenant il habite quelque chose d'intelligible. Il lui convient d'échapper au hasard par la géométrie. Voici par lui à la rencontre des deux diamètres et des deux diagonales le centre qui est devenu conscient de lui-même. (*Oc,* XXV, 244.)

In keeping with this, Claudel likens the human psyche to a

walnut, «[ce] fruit intellectuel par excellence» (*Oc,* XXII, 280), for the walnut which looks like a brain is divided into four parts. The poet also tells us: «Notre âme à sa table est assise au centre, au foyer d'une quadruple introversion. C'est la figure et le domaine de la vie intérieure. C'est notre cellule» (*Oc,* XXI, 199). Finally, we can link this internal structure to the famous muses of Claudel's maturity—«les Quatre grandes Extérieures ... les grandes Muses carrées» (*Opo,* 285). It is they who guard the four doors of his inner habitation.

Claudel is of course not alone in his interest in numbers and their significance. Carl Jung is also known to have been fascinated by this subject. It is he who said: «Number helps more than anything else to bring order into the chaos of appearances. It is the predestined instrument for creating order ... It may well be the most primitive element of order in the human mind, seeing that the numbers one to four occur with the greatest frequency and have the widest incidence. In other words, primitive patterns of order are mostly triads or tetrads» (8).

Concerning the quaternity he adds: «[It] is one of the most widespread archetypes and has also proved to be one of the most useful schemata for representing the arrangment of functions by which the conscious mind takes its bearings» (9). He also teaches: «The quaternity ... forms the logical basis for any whole judgement. ... Schopenhauer proves that the 'Principle of Sufficient Reason' has a fourfold root. This is because the fourfold aspect is the minimum requirement for a complete judgement» (10). Then: «The quaternity is

---

(8) Carl G. Jung, *The Structure and Dynamics of the Psyche,* trans. by R. F. C. Hull, Bollingen Series XX (New York City: Pantheon Books, 1960), p. 456.

(9) Carl G. Jung, *The Practice of Psychotherapy: Essays on the Psychology of Transference and Other Subjects,* trans. by R. F. C. Hull, Bollingen Series XX (New York City: Pantheon Books, 1966), p. 207.

(10) Carl G. Jung, *Psychology and Religion: West and East,*

an organizing schema par excellence, something like the cross-threads of a telescope. It is a system of co-ordinates that is used almost instinctively for dividing up and arranging a chaotic multiplicity» (11). Finally, and perhaps most important, we hear it said: «The quaternity ... always represents a consciously reflected and differentiated totality. Quite apart from its almost universal incidence it also appears spontaneously in dreams as an expression of the total personality» (12). If we apply these last two remarks to Claudel and his avowedly chaotic psychic state, we will understand the importance of the quaternity in his plays, which we know to be the products of involuntary psychic activity («Avec le drame nous pénétrons dans la région la plus obscure du cerveau humain celle du rêve» [*Opr*, 52-53]).

The quaternity is undoubtedly the dominant structure in Claudel's theatre—the structure that implies totality. It appears in several forms and on several levels. If we examine his plays we notice that the great majority are composed of either three or four acts. (The only two-act plays written by Claudel are *Protée*, a satire in which everyone is half-god and half-beast, and *Le Livre de Christophe Colomb*, a play with two heroes or one hero divided against himself —Christophe Colomb I and Christophe Colomb II.) But only those plays made up of four acts (*L'Annonce faite à Marie, Le Soulier de satin* and *Le Père humilié* are considered to be definitive statements. Only they seem to offer some viable solution to the poet's inner struggles or reveal a poet at peace with himself (even if the peace is transitory and the solution ultimately unsatisfactory). *L'Annonce faite à Marie,* for instance, is called «un drame qui boucle, dont tous les

————
trans. by R. F. C. Hull, 2nd ed., Bollingen Series XX (Princeton: Princeton University Press, 1963), p. 167.

(11) Carl G. Jung, *Aion: Researches into the Phenomenology of the Self*, trans. by R. F. C. Hull, Bollingen Series XX (New York City: Pantheon Books, 1959), p. 242.

(12) Jung, *Mysterium*, p. 203.

différents éléments se composent et finissent convenablement» (*Mi*, 273). Of *Le Soulier de satin* it is said: «Toute l'oeuvre est basée sur un sentiment de triomphe, d'enthousiasme, d'être venu à bout d'une situation très difficile, d'avoir trouvé l'équilibre» (*Mi*, 322). Finally, if we examine *Le Père humilié* we see that in and through it the poet has indeed achieved a certain equilibrium. In comparison with the condition betrayed in the first two plays of the trilogy, here, he is relatively at peace. As a result, the atmosphere of this play is not, as it was in *L'Otage* and *Le Pain dur*, «une atmosphère de mécontentement, de regrets, de remords, de nostalgie, de douleur qui est tout à fait particulière» (*Mi*, 299). Yet we must admit that *Le Père humilié* does not furnish a totally satisfactory conclusion to the trilogy. Claudel himself says: «Dans ma pensée, ce drame n'épuisait pas d'ailleurs la destinée d'une lignée représentative. Then he adds: «J'attendais de l'inspiration le cadeau d'un quatrième et dernier évènement» (*T*, II, 1455) and with this we grasp the problem—the series itself is incomplete. It should have been a tetralogy rather than a trilogy. «Ces trois drames ... évidemment, comportent une conclusion et un couronnement ... Ce que j'appellerai une 'piece de consommation' réalisant les diverses tendances, divergentes ou convergentes, si on aime mieux, qui se manifestent dans les trois premières pièces. Il s'agissait, somme toute, de donner une conclusion à ces conflits étendus dont les trois premières pièces sont l'expression et le théâtre, et j'ai été incapable de le trouver» (*Mi*, 285). As we know, *Le Soulier de satin* was to be the conclusion to the trilogy as well as the crowning piece of Claudel's entire theatrical production.

At this point one might well ask: If the above is true, why is the play *L'Histoire de Tobie et de Sara*, which was obviously written by a man basically at peace with himself, in three parts rather than four? The reason for this stems from the inherent nature of the numbers three and four as described by Claudel. Three is the number of divine virtue or spiritual totality, whereas four expresses human totality.

8

L'Histoire de Tobie et de Sara is in three parts because it deals exclusively with the sacred drama and Biblical characters who are symbolic of divine personages. The rest of Claudel's plays, however, are obviously in three acts for another reason —they do not express human totality or equilibrium.

More important than all of this is the role played by the quaternity on the level of characterization within each of Claudel's plays. Even superficial investigation will reveal that most of Claudel's plays have four main characters. Many of them, of course, also have many other characters—revealing the poet's inner multiplicity—but this ofttimes chaotic multitude usually depends upon and is in someway organized around a quartet of main characters. (We should remark in passing that the quaternion of psychic elements which these four characters inevitably represent is present in both *L'Otage* and *La Jeune Fille Violaine* [first version] in another mode. Claudel instructs that the action of these two plays take place in rooms—which we now know to represent inner space— each with four windows, or four ways of looking out.)

This quartet invariably takes one of two forms. Either it is composed of two men and two women, as in *Tête d'Or*, *L'Annonce faite à Marie, L'Échange, Protée* and *Le Pain dur* or it is composed of three men and one woman, as in *La Ville, Partage de midi, L'Otage, Le Père humilié* and *Le Soulier de satin*. In each play the members of the quaternion can be distinguished from other characters by their dominant role and by the fact that they all interact sexually. The two exceptions are Badilon in *L'Otage* and the Pope in *Le Père humilié*. They are both included in their respective quaternions, however, because they are intimately involved in the love relations of the other characters. The formulation 2 + 2 (two men and two women) occurs primarily in those plays written or conceived prior to 1900, that is, prior to Claudel's encounter with Rosalie L. This is highly significant in that the switch from a 2 + 2 structure to a 3 + 1 format (three men and one woman) translates a new perspective with regard to women on Claudel's part.

In his early plays Claudel's conception of women is split. (*La Ville* is the only exception.) His Anima has two radically different, though obviously compensatory, aspects which are represented by two opposing females. On the one hand we have Galaxaure, the Princess, Violaine and Marthe—spiritual, ethereal femininity; and on the other we have Strombo, Tête d'Or's first wife, Mara and Lechy—earth-bound, primitive, even evil womanhood. (That these two types of women represent two sides of the same psychic whole is especially apparent in the pair Violaine/Mara. Together they are compared to a single fruit. Violaine is the delicious exterior pulp and Mara the hard interior nut.) After 1900 these two aspects of femininity seem to meld in the poet's unconscious and he conceives women such as Ysé, Sygne, Pensée and Prouhèze—women much more complex than those mentioned above because they are more complete. (To reconfirm our view that Claudel's conception of woman did change at this point we need only consider that in the two plays written after 1900 which are structured 2 + 2—*Le Pain dur* and *Protée*—the classic Claudelian conflict of feminine opposites is no longer in evidence. Neither Lumîr nor Sichel is saintly or truly evil and the same can be said of Brindosier and Hélène.) Sygne, Pensée, Ysé and Prouhèze might then all be said to represent a synthesis of opposites, and for that reason they are all essentially ambiguous in nature. They are endowed with some sense of the spiritual, yet they sin.

As we might suspect, Jung has something to say concerning this type of change in consciousness. In the following passages he discusses the nature of the psychological functions and the shift in the structure of a quaternion from 2 + 2 to 3 + 1. First we learn: «In the psychology of the functions [in a man] there are two conscious and therefore masculine functions, the differentiated function and its auxiliary, which are represented in dreams by, say, father and son, whereas the unconscious functions appear as mother and daughter». Then we are told: «It is possible for the third function—that is, the unconscious auxiliary one—to be raised to consciousness and thus made masculine. It will, however, bring with it traces of its contamination [union] with the inferior function, thus acting as a kind of link with the darkness of the unconscious» (13). With this we ask: Could we not gauge Claudel's psychological condition, the level of consciousness revealed in his plays, by these Jungian standards in which femininity is linked with the unconscious (especially since Claudel himself tells us that woman is the unknown)?

Let us begin by examining L'Endormie, the poet's first play, in which his level of consciousness is at its lowest point. This is evidenced by the fact that we have here as many as three important female characters. Furthermore, one of these women is asleep throughout the play, which indicates that she has not yet fully emerged in the poet's psyche. Another is in a cave—her condition is pre-natal. Unconsciousness still prevails.

Tête d'Or Claudel's first major work, should reveal a rise in the plane of consciousness. We see that it does. We notice that one of the women—Tête d'Or's first wife—is barely developed and that the two men both seem «contaminated» by unconscious elements. (We hear Cébès complain: «Mais je suis comme un homme sous terre dans un endroit où on n'entend rien. / Qui ouvrira la porte? et qui descendra vers moi dans la demeure où je suis, portant le feu jaune dans la main?» [T, I, 180]. This yellow light is the light of consciousness.) Consequently, both have feminine characteristics. This is apparent in Cébès, who is anything but manly, but with Tête d'Or, that super-masculine hero, the contamination is less apparent. Yet we hear him call himself «mère meilleure». Then he adds: «Si quelqu'un de vous m'appelle femme à cause de ces cheveux longs, il est vrai!» (T, I, 98) and: «Qui dit que je suis une femme? / Certes, je suis une vierge farouche et sur qui on ne mettra

---

(13) Carl G. Jung, Psychology and Alchemy, trans. by R. F. C. Hull, 2nd ed., Bollingen Series XX (Princeton: Princeton University Press, 1968), p. 152.

pas la main aisément! / En effet je suis une femme, regardez quelle femme je suis!» (*T*, I, 238). We also hear him say: «Mes entrailles s'emeuvent comme celles d'une mère!» (*T*, I, 80) and: «Que veux-tu de moi? Est-ce que je te cacherai dans mon ventre et est-ce que je t'enfanterai de nouveau?» (*T*, I, 220). We know too that after the battle he smiles «le sourire perfide de la jeune fille!» (*T*, I, 75). Finally, he cries «gouttelettes de femme» (*T*, I, 80) and we hear Cébès call him: «Mère, mon frère! ô ma nourrice aux côtes cuirassées!» (*T*, I, 84).

Tête d'Or's radical rejection of femininity can now be better understood in psychological terms as the by-product of his struggle for consciousness—a struggle which inevitably and necessarily entails a rejection of the very element which would overwhelm him. «Moi-même, je suis dans ce lieu profond!» he cries—but then adds: «Je me lèverai et j'enfoncerai la porte et j'apparaîtrai devant les hommes!» (*T*, I, 181). He wills to breaks out of the maternal womb of the unconscious and into the light.

By the time we get to *L'Échange* the poet's psychic situation shows marked improvement. His degree of consciousness has risen—here, we have two fully developed women characters. What's more, only one of the masculine figures seems to be «contaminated» by feminine traits—Louis Laine of whom Claudel says: «C'est lui ... qui est Anima» (*T*, I, 1305).

Finally, with *Partage de midi* the shift occurs. Consciousness is augmented, Claudel's vision of woman is unified and we switch to the 3 + 1 format. But we note, as per Jung's description of the process, that one of the figures in what is now a masculine trio has obviously just recently emerged from the feminine domaine of the unconscious. So we hear Ysé say of De Ciz: «Il a des yeux de femme tout à fait» (*T*, I, 991), and: «Je suis un homme! je l'aime comme on aime une femme!» (*T*, I, 1006).

These same observations might also be made concerning *Le Soulier de satin*. Here, Camille is the «contaminated» third member of the masculine trio, and as such he confesses: «Il y a de la femme en moi» (*T*, II, 773). He is the poet's shadow and does indeed act «as a kind of a link with the darkness of the unconscious». It is for this reason that he is portrayed by the poet as being a character of swarthy complexion whose domain is understandably to the south, in Africa with Prouhèze.

There is yet another way in which the quaternion is present in Claudel's works. It is in connection with the children that appear throughout his theatre. These children inevitably represent a synthesis of three opposing strains, and through them we are again confronted with a 3 + 1 structure. The example that first comes to mind is the infant in *L'Annonce faite à Marie* who is actually born of Mara, Jacques, and Violaine. There are many such children. There is Ivors, born of Lala and Coeuvre but apparently brought up by Avare. There is Marthe and Louis' baby who will be reared by Thomas. (Claudel says that the baby needs Thomas to be fulfilled.) Mesa and Ysé's child comes under the tutelage of Amalric. Pensée's infant has Orian for a father, but Orso for a step-father. Pensée herself is the product of three races. She is the grand-daughter of Turelure and Sygne and the daughter of Louis and Sichel. We even discover that this same format is present in a third version of *Tête d'Or* composed in 1949. Tête d'Or's first companion was to have had a child by Cébès (14).

This type of interaction is to be expected when we recall that all of these characters are but varying representatives of the poet's developing inner reality. Recollection of this fact is also important in any attempt to explain the ambiguities of the theme of love at first sight. Many may wonder why the language of fascination (see Chapter II) is used so indiscriminately in Claudel's plays. One might ask: How can

_____

(14) Petit, *Claudel et l'usurpateur*, p. 65.

Lechy, for instance, claim to be made for Louis when Marthe, who is his legitimate wife, makes similar claims? Or, who is Prouhèze really meant for—Camille or Rodrigue? If Jacques is to be joined with Violaine in the after-life, what happens to Mara his legal wife to whom salvation is also offered? What of Turelure's claims on Sygne and Sichel's on Louis? How can the actress tell Rodrigue that she recognizes him? But such questions are easily resolved when we realize that all of these characters are representations of Claudel's psychic being which he seeks to unify by accepting each of its facets. Seen in this light, the situation seems altered. We can understand why Turelure has as much right to Sygne as Georges does, why Lechy claims Louis, and so on.

Perhaps the most important child in Claudel's theatre is Sept-Épées—the offspring of Camille, Prouhèze, and Rodrigue who is called «cet enfant merveilleux» (T, II, 1475). Interestingly enough, her significance lies in her sex. Although in many ways she appears to be androgynous (and in so far as she is, she represents a union of opposites), she is of course a young woman. Up to this point all the children mentioned would seem to have been boys, with the exception of Aubaine (formerly Aubin in La Jeune Fille Violaine), and Pensée, a figure whose full significance is difficult to judge, however, due to the incomplete state of the trilogy. We can only guess at her importance for Claudel from remarks such as the following which the poet makes concerning his proposed addition to the trilogy: «Tout ce que je sais, c'est que cette nouvelle pièce aurait tourné autour d'une Pensée très agée, disons agée de soixante-dix ans, qui aurait eu un rôle, mon Dieu, de Pythie ... qui aurait réuni en elle l'explication de toutes ces agitations passées, en même temps qu'une ouverture sur l'avenir» (T, II, 1452).

If we take the appearance of the child to symbolize a type of rebirth, we realize that in Sept-Épées (as with Aubaine) the poet has at last accepted his femininity, his soul or, on another level, his unconscious. He now identifies with her.

He identifies with that female principle in and through which he will be united with God. He has surrendered to his spirituality.

This surrender or acceptance is also denoted by the fact that in later versions of his plays—those written after 1924, the date of the completion of *Le Soulier de satin*—we see Claudel make a distinct effort to «rehabilitate» his female characters. This is done with Mara. In the 1938 version of the fourth act of *L'Annonce faite à Marie,* Anne for the first time accepts Mara as a part of himself and suggests that she isn't really as bad as she seems. He suggests that she was possessed when she committed her crimes. «Non, Mara, ce n'est pas toi, c'est un autre qui te possédait. Mara, mon enfant! tu souffres et je voudrais te consoler! / Il est revenu à la fin, il est à toi pour toujours ce père jadis que tu aimais! / Mara, Violaine! ô mes deux petites filles! ô mes deux petits enfants dans mes bras! Toutes les deux, je vous aimais et vos coeurs ensemble ne faisaient qu'un avec le mien!» (*T,* II, 213). Through Anne it is the poet who accepts Mara as part of himself. But not only he; God also accepts Mara through Anne: «Tout vieillard, tout père, est une image de Dieu» (*Opr,* 436). We also see the same rehabilitating process take place with Lechy, Ysé and even Marthe. The poet has come to terms with his Anima. He no longer fears her. As a result she loses her more fearful and undesirable characteristics.

Returning now to our discussion of the quaternion, we note that there is one figure which has been conspicuous by its absence: the emblem of Christianity—the cross, the importance of which we will now examine.

The cross in Claudel's universe is a principle of division. As such it is not something to be eschewed, however. Quite the contrary, for Claudel recognizes the value of its destructive role. The cross effects a necessary breaking of the old man, «comme l'arbre qu'on crucifie pour fructifier!» (*T,* I, 165). It is the instrument which imparts the death that leads to new life. Then on a psychological level, it also introduces the division and opposition which lead to greater consciousness. «De même toutes nos facultés nous demeurent comme inconnues, et parmi tous nos vains tracas nous avons cette sensation de néant qui accompagne l'oisiveté, si nous n'embrassons cette croix qui nous tend de toutes parts jusqu'à l'extrême» (*Oc*, XV, 133). Claudel also says: «L'angle, c'est ce point où deux lignes en se coupant se prêtent force du fait de leur opposition. C'est l'angle qui donne au tout forme et figure. C'est pourquoi N.-S. est appelé *la pierre angulaire*. Quatre angles réunis par le sommet, c'est la Croix» (*Oc*, XXVI, 31). And then: «Voici par lui à la rencontre des deux diamètres et des deux diagonales le centre qui est devenu conscient de lui-même» (*Oc*, XXV, 244).

Finally, Claudel sums up: «Mais qu'y faire? Admettre sans doute que tout accord est l'effet non pas seulement d'une géometrie, mais d'une lutte, et que la vérité est faite de tendances dans des directions opposées, ou plutôt de coordonnées non pas opposées, mais perpendiculaires—comme la croix. C'est cette idée de vérités qui se rejoignent non pas dans un équilibre statique, mais dans un effort autour d'un point commun et sur des points divergents, qui sert de noeud à toute mon entreprise intellectuelle» (*Oc*, XX, 428).

The cross is then an instrument of salvation through division. But it also surpasses this function and finally unifies what it divided—but on a higher plane. Christ's presence is accompanied by «une vertu unificatrice ... qui réduit les deux parties de notre nature anarchique aux lois de la croix et de la perpendiculaire» (*Oc*, XIX, 144). This reference to a vertical movement is essential—but it can only be understood if we take the following into account: «La direction verticale, [est] celle qui rassemble, celle qui compose, celle qui permet au regard entre les quatre points cardinaux de marier les différents aspects de l'étendue» (*Oc*, XXI, 487). It is by means of this vertical pull that all creatures will be drawn to their end which is God.

With this in mind we can now understand why Camille in *Le Soulier de satin,* for instance, raises Prouhèze's arm, holding her hand in his, or why at the end of *L'Annonce faite à Marie* Anne lifts the hands of Mara and Jacques. «Il a appris que ce n'est qu'en élevant que l'on réconcilie» (*T*, II, 1396). In another version of this same play we also see Mara lift her baby, with whom she traces the sign of the cross. This is a symbol of integration, both psychic and otherwise. The sign of the cross, like the cross itself, like all vertical movement, is a sign of unity. «Le signe de la croix, c'est-à-dire l'ascension de la main qui part du creux de la poitrine, monte au front, redescend au coeur, vient à gauche et puis à droite atteindre sur chacune de nos épaules l'origine de nos mouvements et actes physiques et enveloppe, pour ainsi dire, dans un cycle vérificateur à la fois de notre création et attestateur de notre salut, les quatre points cardinaux de la personne humaine» (*T*, II, 1518). Like Mara, Joan of Arc also makes this gesture—with her two hands bound, indicating on yet another level the union of right and left through the cross.

Even for the lovers in Claudel's theatre it is only on the cross that union is really possible. It is only here that the opposites can truly be united—left and right, feminine and masculine, east and west—whether they be opposites within or opposites without. So we see the cross termed a nuptial bed—the site of union and reconciliation. Claudel says: «De cette énergie incessante du Christ qui tire tout à Lui, de ce quadruple désir qui s'exerce à la fois sur la gauche et sur la droite, sur l'altitude et sur la profondeur, de cette Unité unificatrice, de cette opération cosmique, la croix est non seulement le symbole abstrait, mais si j'osais dire, l'expression mécanique» (*Oc,* XIX, 397).

On another plane, we discover that the cross is «la sublime intersection en qui le ciel est joint à la terre par l'homme» (*T,* I, 844). With this one of Claudel's favorite images comes to mind—the tree which he associates with both man and the cross because like them the tree through its branches and roots unites heaven and earth, the above and the below, the masculine and the feminine, yang and yin.

The importance of the cross with its power to reconcile opposites becomes apparent when we realize that a yearning for unity was undoubtedly the most deep-seated longing in Claudel's life, and this on all levels. All of his theatrical production was an effort to achieve this end, an effort to unite the various facets of his psyche. But it was only with *Le Soulier de satin* that he seems to have achieved his final goal. We saw one aspect of this when we discussed the importance of Sept-Épées. But triumph in her was only possible because in this play Camille attains what Tête d'Or and Turelure, for instance, were not able fully to attain in other plays—salvation, which was the product of sacrifice and the cross, or, on another plane, of the acceptance on the part of all the characters involved of Camille's worth *tel quel*. This means two things. On the one hand that God—in Prouhèze—has been forced into accepting all of Claudel or Claudel just as he is, and on the other, that Claudel himself has succeeded in dealing with, in accepting, all parts of his inner being, no matter how dark or nefarious. He is whole. Prior efforts to achieve wholeness were always somehow thwarted or incomplete. It is only after having written *Le Soulier de satin* that the poet was able to say: «Toute l'oeuvre est basée sur un sentiment de triomphe, d'enthousiasme, d'être venue à bout d'une situation difficile, d'avoir trouvé l'équilibre» (*Mi*, 322). It was also only after having written *Le Soulier de satin* that he was able to reconcile himself with Mara.

That this psychic integration was indispensable, that acceptance by Claudel of all facets of his being was necessary, becomes clear when we hear him say: «Que rien d'humain ne soit soustrait à notre jouissance!» (*T*, I, 463) or: «Je ne crois pas qu'il faille abandonner aucune de ces facultés que Dieu nous a données en faveur d'une autre» (*Mi*, 164). Then finally: «Il y a autour de moi une réquisition, une urgence infinie que je sois, aussi complètement et intensément que je peux, moi-même!» (*Oc*, XXIII, 234).

But Claudel is also concerned with unity and wholeness

on a more cosmic scale. As a poet he is exhorted: «Réunis mystérieusement, poëte, ces choses qui gémissent d'être séparées» (*Opo,* 684), and also: «Réunis le monde en un seul vers qui cesse d'être dès qu'on l'a dit. / Expire-la tout entière enfin d'un seul coup, cette image transitoire de ce qui ne peut passer! / Rends à Dieu son univers complet dans sa forme et dans sa moralité» (*Opo,* 685). His duty is to God and to that task which he has been given: Unite all things in Him!

Commands such as these call to mind Claudel's conquering heroes: Tête d'Or who says: «Je réunirai tout ce qu'il y a de mâle autour de moi» (*T,* I, 240), and: «En cela que quelque chose ne m'est pas soumis, je ne suis pas libre» (*T,* I, 96); Rodrigue who affirms: «J'ai rompu un continent par le milieu et ... ai passé deux mers ... pour que toutes les parties de l'humanité soient réunies» (*T,* II, 871); Christopher Columbus: «C'est lui qui a réuni la Terre Catholique et en a fait un seul globe au-dessous de la Croix» (*T,* II, 1132); and finally, Joan of Arc: «la grande 'réunisseuse' de notre Pays» (*Oc,* XIV, 280).

But Claudel's vision of unity extends even beyond these vast limits, In an extraordinary passage he informs us: «Comme Satan est un principle de discorde, la voici, elle, [Marie] qui d'un bout à l'autre de la Création est un principe, une puissance de réunion, à quoi l'enfer lui-même se montrera incapable d'échapper. Ce révolté qui ne veut pas servir, est-ce que Son maître va lui permettre de ne servir à rien? C'est sa haine, c'est sa volonté de disruption et de divergence qui va être adroitement employée à la consolidation de toutes choses dans le Christ. Oui, toutes choses! c'est bien le terme dont use l'apôtre, une totalité à quoi l'enfer lui-même est partie. Dieu l'oblige à être à jamais l'instrument de Son dessein. Tout désormais est uni par un lien indissoluble. C'est Satan, par la main de cette séduite qui se tend là-haut vers le fruit, qui a obtenu l'Incarnation» (*Oc,* XXV, 537). Here obviously we encounter once again a 3 + 1 structure representing totality—the Triune God opposed by the Devil.

The above passage is important, but not only because of what it says concerning the principle of evil. It is also important because of what it suggests concerning Claudel's concept of unity, a concept further elucidated in the following: «Ce que nous appelions une muraille est précisément le lien, la communication supersubstantielle qui nous unit, la bienheureuse séparation qui nous permet d'être un en étant deux. Nous refusons à Dieu cette disparition de nous-mêmes en Lui qui nous permettrait de ne pas être là pour L'aimer. Nous ne viendrons pas à bout l'un de l'autre. Nous sommes unifiés non par la fusion, mais par la différence. Nous puisons bienheureusement l'un dans l'autre nos raisons à jamais de différer. Nous sommes constitués ensemble non pas dans l'inertie et dans la mort, mais dans l'énergie, dans cet amour que j'appellerai absurdement un antagonisme inépuisable» (Oc, XXII, 192). Pictured here is a type of union which obviously implies separation. This of course reminds us of what was said in Chapter II (p. 45-46) concerning man's union with woman which we know to be symbolic of his union with God. We see now, as we saw then, that Claudel feared any union in which he might be required to surrender himself completely. He would not relinquish his personal identity. For this reason, union in this mind is not a melding but rather a sort of dynamic equilibrium, the type of thing produced by a love described in the following terms: «Or qu'est-ce l'amour sinon cet acte, cette trouvaille, qui en restant deux nous permet de devenir un seul? C'est le poids seul qui nous permet de réaliser cette merveille paradoxale. Mettez en effet deux êtres sur la même balance et l'aiguille ne marquera qu'un seul poids indivisible» (Oc, XXIV, 268). This image of the scales appears frequently in Claudel's works. It suggests a unity like the one produced by two vowels combining to form a diphthong.

On a psychological level, it might be said that what Claudel fears is a return to unconsciousness, to a unity which, because it is undifferentiated, is unaware of itself: «Toute la création s'est faite par un travail de séparation et de discernement» (*Oc,* XX, 315), and then: «Il faut se diviser pour comprendre» (*Oc,* XXIII, 300), or, on another level, he speaks of procuring «par la résistance de l'autre conscience de soi» (*Oc,* XXIII, 346). All of which would seem to imply that undifferentiated wholeness is synonymous with unconscious wholeness—a state which the Gnostics of old identified with the «non-existent all-being» (15), a state which Claudel rejects. And it is undoubtedly for this reason that even after having achieved psychic integration in *Le Soulier de satin,* psychic division—but without hostility—is still present in the poet's creative production. We need only recall the many characters in his last plays and prose writings who have doubles like Christopher Columbus and Joan of Arc.

Claudel's model for unity is, as it should be for a Christian, the Triune God. God the Father sent His Son to the earth and «le commandement, le conseil, la supplication qu'Il L'a chargé d'apporter aux hommes, c'est *d'être Un, comme Nous, dit-il, Nous sommes Un*» (Oc, XXIV, 259-60). Here we are ideed presented with a differentiated unity, but still a unity far beyond anything Claudel was willing or able to attempt.

Now that we have considered what unity meant to Claudel, let us examine some of the things he tells us will help achieve this unity. We have already studied the prime uniting force in Claudel's universe—Christ and His cross. We also encountered Mary as a uniting principle in one of the above quotations and this naturally reminded us that woman, representing either Mary, Sophia, the Church, or the city is also a uniting and reconciling force. Then too we recall that the poet, his mind, his voice, and his words—all were said to possess powers that unite. But what are some

(15) Carl G. Jung, *Civilization in Transition,* trans. by R. F. C. Hull, Bollingen Series XX (New York City: Pantheon Books, 1964), p. 407.

of the other things to which Claudel attributes this synthesizing virtue?

Our first grouping of these forces might include: faith, which is said to unite the two parts of creation—the visible and the invisible; penitence, which Ysé tells us is like cement uniting good and evil; prayer, of which Claudel has this to say: «La prière est un acte de maturité indispensable au complet développement de la personnalité, l'ultime intégration des facultés de l'homme les plus hautes. C'est seulement en priant que nous achevons cette union complète et harmonieuse du corps, de l'intelligence et de l'âme qui confère au frêle roseau humain sa force» (*Oc,* XXIII, 67); and finally suffering and sacrifice, the efficacy of which is described as follows: «De ces rapports entre Dieu et l'homme la condition déterminante est une certaine rupture de cet état d'équilibre où ils peuvent se passer l'un de l'autre, et l'instrument matériel est le sacrifice» (*Oc,* XXIII, 406). Love is also a uniting force as are beauty, goodness, truth, and praise: «La louange est *par excellence* le thème qui compose. Personne ne chante seul. Même les étoiles du Ciel ... chantent ensemble» (*Opr,* 64).

On another level, we know that fire (symbolic of the Holy Spirit) serves to unite. Blood is called the vehicle and instrument of unity. Liquids of all kinds, in fact, are one of Claudel's most important unifying symbols. We are all said to have an inner humidity which is associated with the soul, the spirit and even intelligence. It is this inner humidity that unites us with God: «Mon âme, par tout ce qu'il y a en moi d'humide je touche à Dieu!» (*Opo,* 696). Claudel speaks of «cette humidité secrète par quoi / Toutes les âmes d'hommes / Adhèrent d'une certaine manière, en sorte qu'un même vent les ébranle / Comme une onde qui se propage» (*T,* I, 645), and with this Jung's collective unconscious comes to mind, which, like Claudel's sea, appears to men as a feminine principle of creativity.

Other unifying forces also exist: music (Claudel speaks of «tout ce que l'Humanité réussit à mettre ensemble ... pour

répondre à l'obscure invitation de la musique» [*Opr,* 644])
and perfume («Je suis envahie par un parfum qui me permet
de dire Nous [*Opr,* 731]).   Then there is the morning star
which is also the evening star «qui ... ne cesse de coudre
la journée qui finit à celle qui commence» (*Oc,* XVI, 425)
and the moon that has both a light and dark side and is said
to unite all contradictions.   The moon, of course, is feminine
as we saw in Chapter I (p. 8).   She is associated with
Mary (as is the star mentioned above) and is said to draw
all things to herself.   Even the sea is under her dominion.
She reigns over the night world—the world of sleep, dreams
and fantasy and her light is a musical instrument of unity.
Claudel tells of a harmony which resembles moonlight through
which the heavens are joined to the earth.   And in this
connection let us not forget that Double Shadow in *Le Soulier
de satin* was formed by the light of the moon.

There is yet another essential unifying principle without
which union of any kind would actually be impossible.   This
factor is the all-important void.   Claudel explains: «Lucifer
seul s'est considéré comme parfait et compact et il est tombé
aussitôt, comme une pierre, par son propre poids.   C'est
parce que toutes les choses créées sont imparfaites, c'est parce
qu'il y a en elles un certain manque, un certain vide radical,
—qu'elles respirent, qu'elles vivent, qu'elles échangent, qu'elles
ont besoin de Dieu et des autres créatures, qu'elles se prêtent
à toutes les combinaisons de la poésie et de l'amour» (*Opr,*
433-34).

With this we may begin discussing the importance of the
circle, for in Claudel's mind the circle and void come together
in the form of a zero.   «O, c'est un miroir, à moins que ce
ne soit le vide parfait et le rond de l'âme dilatée vers l'esprit
oral» (*Oc,* XX, 39).   The circle is a uniting symbol as we
see when we consider the virtue of the wedding band, for
instance, which serves to unite man and woman in marriage,
or when we consider the consequences of a simple «Oui».
«Tout est transformé pour nous en ce Oui tout rond, en cette
pièce de monnaie que nous n'avons qu'à ouvrir la main pour

céder, afin que ce qui est du côté de l'homme dénuement réponde à ce qui est du côté de Dieu gratuité, et que avec Rien nous achetons Tout» (*Oc,* XIX, 264). We should also recall the iron ring that united Joan of Arc's two hands. It, like the marriage band, symbolically joins right and left, yang and yin.

But the circle also has even broader significance for Claudel. In addition to associating it with voids, zeros, mirrors, the soul, rings and «oui», the poet also identifies it with eggs, semen, the sun, holes, the face, the moon, wheels, pulleys, an open mouth, lakes, islands, nuts, open windows, and finally Chinese vases.

We should note that many of these things are feminine: the soul, voids, since they are yin, and Chinese vases—all of which were identified with each other in Chapter I (p. 15). There, too, it was said that Sophia was connected with ovals which suggest eggs, and that Mary was identified with mirrors and the moon. But other round objects are also associated with the feminine quaternion of Chapter I. There is the church whose interior is likened to a womb and the enclosed city, «une cité dans son enceinte pareille au rond de la bouche» (*Opo,* 274). Then we have the other symbol-attributes of Mary—the fountain, the rose, the rosary, and the enclosed garden, which takes on cosmic proportions: «Il s'était arrangé pour gagner, pour saisir entre Ses doigts cette petite boule, la nôtre, dont Il voulait faire en soufflant dessus, le hortus conclusus de Sa Bien-Aimée» (*Oc,* XXV, 536). From this we gather that the earth itself is feminine. Finally, we should note that many of these allegories of femininity are ambiguous in character like Anima herself. The moon has its dark side as do mirrors. The enclosed garden can be a place of sin and suffering. And of the rose it is said: «Certain of the ecclesiastical symbols prove to be acutely dualistic, and this is also true of the rose. Above all it is an allegory of Mary and of various virtues. Its perfume is the odour of sanctity, as in the case of St. Elizabeth and St. Teresa. At the same time it symbolizes human beauty [*venustas*], indeed the lust of the world [*voluptas mundi*]» (16). So in Claudel's mind the Rose is both Mary and Ysé.

The circle is also intimately connected with the quaternity and the cross: «X c'est d'abord un carrefour, la pointe de rencontre de quatre directions ... Les quatre angles que ses deux branches déterminent constituent le principe de toute géometrie plane, tandis que devenant ailes par la rotation ils créent la sphère» (*Oc*, XVIII, 458). Then: «Le carré, nous le voyons partout exister dans la sphère» (*Oc*, XXV, 246) and we are reminded that Chinese coins, for instance, have this shape. They are circular and have a square hole in the middle. This configuration apparently symbolizes a union of opposites, for Claudel tells us that in Chinese philosophy the circle is said to represent the heavens which are yang and the square, the earth which is yin.

For a psychological interpretation of the importance of the circle and its relation to the square we will turn to Jung. First he informs us that the circle or mandala (the Indian term for the circles drawn in religious rituals) is a symbol of wholeness. It is in fact «the simplest symbol of wholeness and therefore the simplest God image» (17). (We recall the famous definition—God is an infinite circle [or sphere] whose center is everywhere and the circumference nowhere.) He also tells us that mandalas have «a distinct tendancy toward quadripartite structure» (18). Then, concerning «the famous mediaeval problem of the squaring of the circle which belongs to the sphere of alchemy» (to which Claudel alluded above and to which Jung attributes psychological significance): «The total personality is indicated by the four cardinal points of

---

(16) Jung, *Mysterium*, p. 306.

(17) Carl G. Jung, *Alchemical Studies*, trans. by R. F. C. Hull, Bollingen Series XX (Princeton: Princeton University Press, 1967), p. 337.

(18) Carl G. Jung, Foreward and Commentary to *The Secret of the Golden Flower: A Chinese Book of Life*, trans. and explained by Richard Wilhelm (New York City: Harcourt, Brace & World, Inc., 1962), p. 100.

the horizon, the four gods, *i.e.* the four functions which give orientation in psychic space, and by the circle enclosing the whole» (19). «[The squared circle is then] a double totality symbol; the circle representing non-differentiated wholeness, and the square discriminated wholeness» (20). Interestingly enough this is reflected in Claudel's theatre. Those plays which have a four-part structure, and only those, are also in some way circular. First we have *Le Soulier de satin* which is a play that begins and ends at the same point—in the middle of the ocean. Then we have *L'Annonce faite à Marie:* «A partir du 1er acte, ça roule, ça tourne rond» (*Mi,* 276).

Jung also has this to say concerning mandalas: «At a certain stage in the psychological treatment patients sometimes paint or draw ... mandalas spontaneously, either because they dream them or because they suddenly feel the need to compensate the confusion in their psyches through representations of an ordered unity» (21). Then, concerning the magic circle: «The idea is to protect what is within from the intrusion and admixture of what is without, as well as to prevent it from escaping» (22). Finally: «The round or square inclosures ... have the value of magic means to produce protective walls or a vas hermeticum to prevent an outburst and a disintegration. Thus the mandala denotes and supports an exclusive concentration upon oneself. This state is anything but egocentricity. It is on the contrary a much needed self-control with the purpose of avoiding inflation and dissociation» (23). Here we have the needed explanation for Claudel's fascination with circles.

After learning all this, we are not startled to hear Tête d'Or say: «Ce monde-ci a été fait pour l'homme et une limite

(19) Jung, *Two Essays*, p. 247.
(20) Jung, *Mysterium*, p. 241.
(21) Jung, *Psychology and Religion: West and East*, p. 574.
(22) Jung, *Psychology and Alchemy*, p. 167.
(23) Jung, *Psychology and Religion* (Yale University Press), p. 105.

a été tracée autour de lui, / Afin qu'il ne sorte pas, et que personne n'entre non plus» (*T*, I, 221). Even Claudel's conquering heroes would stay within the limits of a circle. Their attempts at conquest are in fact merely efforts to unite the earth, to perfect the circle. Such was the case with Christopher Columbus whose wise heart was filled with «la passion de la limite et de la sphère calculée de parfaire l'éternel horizon» (*Opo*, 281). With reason then the cry is heard: «Je pleure la contrée sans baptême / Qui ne peut être atteinte, qui ne peut être fermée par des bornes, ni prise dans les mailles d'un filet» (*T*, I, 123).

Even on a more personal level the poet's reactions are consistent: «Scellez-moi de peur que je ne me dissipe» (*Opo*, 379), then: «Il [le monde] est fermé, et voici soudain que toutes choses à mes yeux ont acquis la proportion et la distance» (*Opo*, 240). He also suggests that we close the doors of our inner room, «car les ténèbres sont extérieures, la lumière est au dedans» (*Opo*, 284).

But the Christian knows that this circle, formed in early manhood when consciousness is being achieved, must be broken—just as the circle of the womb was broken and then later the circle of family and home. And the instrument of this destruction is the cross—represented by woman in Claudel's theatre. This is of course a destruction which the poet resists, primarily because it implies a death, an opening to the unknown, which he fears. But if he would live, he must duplicate Christ's passion, described in the following two passages in terms we can now comprehend: «C'est ce cercle parfait, c'est ce courant d'éternité à travers la chair que la lance du Centurion est venue brutalement traverser et ouvrir» (*Oc*, XX, 116). And: «Mais le cercle n'existe que par une exclusion, par une distance inviolable de la périphérie au centre. Il est une figure de l'immobilité. De quoi c'est Dieu même qui a pris l'initiative de sortir, à condition qu'il obtienne de nous le chemin approprié» (*Oc*, XXIII, 394). So what happened and happens to Christ is this: «Le O emblème de la perfection ... devient Ω oméga, où l'on peut pénétrer» (*J,* II, 509). And this also is what must happen to us. «Il nous faut des trous» (*Oc,* XXII, 190). Our circular reality must be pried open. «Se fendre ... s'ouvrir ... ce déliement ... cette délivrance mystique», but then Rodrigue adds: «Nous savons que nous [en] sommes par nous-mêmes incapables et de là ce pouvoir sur nous de la femme pareil à celui de la Grâce» (*T,* II, 855).

It is also said: «Ce grand trou dans la terre ... que ... fit la Croix lors qu'elle fut plantée. / La voici qui tire tout à elle. / Là est le point qui ne peut être défait, le noeud qui ne peut être dissous, / Le patrimoine commun, la borne intérieure qui ne peut etre arrachée, / Le centre et l'ombilic de la terre, le milieu de l'humanité en qui tout tient ensemble» (*T,* II, 32). This suggests that when we are broken Jesus and His cross will also become our center—a new center for a new reality, a new circular reality «puisque toute forme ne se réalise qu'en s'inscrivant dans le cercle et la sphère» (*Oc,* XXII, 297). We become a new circle, a new vibrating circle whose midpoint is a soul or feminine void which has been united with Jesus, filled with the crucified and risen Jesus. The cross is then the supreme place of encounter and decision, and for this reason it is also called a cross-roads. It occupies the central position in a church and, therefore, also in the circular city that grows up around this church, just as it occupies the central position in the soul, which like the church and city is also feminine. Here the visible and invisible meet. This is the junction of matter and spirit, of the sign and the thing signified, of humanity and God.

The idea that there exists a central point in us and in all things from which there radiates a circle, is most important to Claudel. «O grammarien de mes vers!» he exhorts, «Ne cherche point le chemin, cherche le centre!» (*Opo,* 227). He speaks of a kind of vital point around which all things arrange themselves. In art this mid-point is undoubtedly the mysterious word delivered by the muse—whether it be a visual word or a written word—around which the work develops. And we need only recall what was said in Chapter IV to see the connection between this and the divine reality: «Le Verbe est créateur, tout mot à qui les lèvres de l'homme procurent existence évoque, toute vérité qu'il exprime provoque en vastes zones concentriques une série d'échos» (T, II, 1504). In life this mid-point also represents the moment of birth—the birth of a new man who has been to the cross. So it is that Prouhèze and Rodrigue's sacrifice «produit des conséquences inépuisables, dont la terre seule n'est pas assez large pour parfaire les anneaux divers et concentriques; il faut que le Ciel et l'éternité y viennent ajouter les leurs» (T, II, 1475).

With this we have entered the realm of time, and rightly so, since for each of us the cross represents a moment in time, a moment of decision. In Claudel's poetic universe this central moment is almost always noon. Noon, he tells us, is when Christ died. Noon is when the chaste bride unites with her husband in Solomon's Song, and noon will inevitably be the moment when Claudel's lovers encounter each other authentically, when a decision must be made. It is at noon, in the middle of the ocean, in the middle of his life that Mesa hears Ysé say: «Mesa, je suis Ysé, c'est moi» (T, I, 1339). The sun, considered masculine, unites with the sea and earth at this moment. «Le Soleil en août, quand, gagnant le milieu du ciel, / Il foudroie la mer, il mêle la terre avec lui dans une étreinte aveuglante!» (T, I, 826). (August is of course the mid-point of the year.) This is the moment when the surface of time is broken, just as Christ's body was broken, and eternity penetrates. Finally, it is the moment mirrored in sexual penetration and the orgasm. (Midnight is also the instant of union in Claudel's theatre on occasion. But when this is the case, all passionate, sensual overtones are missing from the picture. The union is spiritual.)

Time itself is linear, but the eternity towards which we are marching is circular. «Nous avançons vers le Royaume de la simultanéité à travers celui de la succession, vers le Festin à travers la Fructification, vers le cercle par le moyen de la ligne» (Oc, XXIV, 229). There are, however, images of this circularity, images of eternity existing even now in time. In fact, with each year that passes «nous complétons ... quelque chose, nous solennisons en douze mois une image de l'éternité» (*Oc,* XXV, 312). A circle is formed, a ring which inevitably suggests the rings of a tree. For this reason the tree is called «un appareil à transformer le temps en permanence» (*Oc,* XXV, 306). Another image of eternity in time is the liturgy, «cette liturgie qui d'un bout de l'année à l'autre décrit autour de nous son cercle informatif» (*Oc,* XXV, 251), a circle which might be termed «un Zodiaque spirituel». Even the face of a clock is round. Finally, this astounding vision of history itself: «Ce n'est pas seulement le passé qui pousse en avant le présent, c'est le futur qui l'aspire: jusqu'à réaliser autour du centre émotif une espèce de lèvre précaire, la crête d'une onde, la surrection liquide d'une espèce d'organe vocal pour le temps d'un certain écho général à proférer, ce qu'on peut appeler le *mot* de la période. Puis le rebord frémissant se dissout et la vague se creuse jusqu'à la formation là-bas d'un nouvel horizon» (*Oc,* XXV, 162). (We might add in passing that all of this brings to mind certain aspects of Jung's theories on causality.)

On yet another level we find that for Claudel all forms are but variations of the circle. The circle in its perfection is the image of both the finite and the infinite. As such, it is the image of man «cet infini conclu dans du fini» (*Oc,* XXII, 296), but also of God who has neither beginning nor end and in whose likeness we were all made finite as He, in His infinite wholeness, is finite. So Claudel says that it is through the finite that we resemble the Infinite. «Soyez béni, mon Dieu, qui ne laissez pas vos oeuvres inachevées / Et qui avez fait de moi un être *fini* à l'image de votre perfection» (*Opo,* 284). (In *Le Livre à venir* Blanchot points to Claudel's extraordinary aversion to the infinite, the unlimited and the indefinite, an aversion which should be understood as a symptom of the poet's psychological fear of dissolution.) Finally, Claudel leaves us with this thought: «L'idée de Cause, et de Cause universelle, c'est-à-dire de toutes parts opératives, ne peut se traduire dans notre esprit que par l'idée de centre, comportant autour de lui un cercle» (*Oc*, XXV, 161).

Our vision of Claudel's universe culminates with a circular reality in which the opposites are united: «Le cercle formé de ces deux figures [yin et yang] constitue pour ainsi dire, par ses transformations, le moteur central de l'univers, il en est l'engin rotatif, l'âme circulaire, la turbine perpétuellement roulante sans frottements et sans déchet» (*Opr*, 1081). Better yet, however, is another version of this same reality, a version more authentic to a European Christian—the double wheel of Ezekiel's vision: «Deux cercles, chacun armé d'un devoir différent et que je me représente sur des plans comme perpendiculaires l'un à l'autre» (*Oc*, XXV, 13). Here we again discover the cross within the circle. Here the opposites are united. The wheels represent time and space, cause and end, existence and expression, permanence and passage, matter and spirit. Furthermore, the whole is an external reality which corresponds to an identical internal reality. Claudel speaks of «le mécanisme mentale (cette roue à l'interieur d'une roue)» (*Oc*, XX, 229). But this is not all. We are also told that this so-called mechanism runs like a clock—a fact that is significant because it recalls a passage in which Mesa says to Ysé: «On marche comme deux montres qui marcheraient l'une par l'autre!» (*Oc*, XI, 344). And with this we discover still another apparition of the double wheel (identical now to Jung's world clock), an apparition which suggests that in it male and female are also finally reconciled.

This circular reality can symbolize none other than the Alpha and Omega, the Beginning and End, the All in All—Christ Jesus.

LIST OF WORKS CITED

Works by Paul Claudel

Claudel, Paul. *Journal.* 2 vols. Bibliothèque de la Pléiade. Paris: Gallimard, 1968-1969.
— *Mémoires improvisés.* Paris: Gallimard, 1969.
— *Oeuvre poétique.* Bibliothèque de la Pléiade. Paris: Gallimard, 1967.
— *Oeuvres complètes.* 26 vols. Paris: Gallimard, 1950-1967.
— *Oeuvres en prose.* Bibliothèque de la Pléiade. Paris: Gallimard, 1965.
— *Théâtre.* 2 vols. Bibliothèque de la Pléiade. Paris: Gallimard, 1965-1967.

Correspondence

Claudel, Paul and Gide, André. *Correspondance, 1899-1926.* 26th ed. Paris: Gallimard, 1949.
— Jammes, Francis and Frizeau, Gabriel. *Correspondance, 1897-1938.* 10th ed. Paris: Gallimard, 1952.
Rivière, Jacques and Claudel, Paul. *Correspondance, 1907-1914.* Paris: Plon-Nourrit et Cie, 1926.
Suarès, André and Claudel, Paul. *Correspondance, 1904-1938.* Paris: Gallimard, 1951.

Works by Carl G. Jung

Jung, Carl G. *Aion: Researches into the Phenomenology of the Self.* Translated by R. F. C. Hull. Bollingen Series XX. New York City: Pantheon Books, 1959.
— *Alchemical Studies.* Translated by R. F. C. Hull. Bollingen Series XX. Princeton: Princeton University Press, 1967.
— *Answer to Job.* Translated by R. F. C. Hull. London: Routledge & Kegan Paul, 1954.
— *The Archetypes and the Collective Unconscious.* 2nd ed. Translated by R. F. C. Hull. Bollingen Series XX. Princeton: Princeton University Press, 1968.
— *Civilization in Transition.* Translated by R. F. C. Hull.

Bollingen Series **XX**. New York City: Pantheon Books, 1964.
— *Contributions to Analytical Psychology*. Translated by H. G. and Cary F. Baynes. London: Kegan Paul, Trench, Trubner & Co. Ltd. New York: Harcourt, Brace and Company, 1928.
— *Mysterium Coniunctionis: An Inquiry into the Separation and Synthesis of Psychic Opposites in Alchemy*. Translated by R. F. C. Hull. Bollingen Series XX. New York City: Pantheon Books, 1968.
— *The Practice of Psychotherapy: Essays on the Psychology of the Transference and Other Subjects*. 2nd ed. Translated by R. F. C. Hull. Bollingen Series XX. New York City: Pantheon Books, 1966.
— *Psychology and Alchemy*. 2nd ed. Translated by R. F. C. Hull. Bollingen Series XX. Princeton: Princeton University Press, 1968.
— *Psychology and Religion*. New Haven: Yale University Press, 1938.
— *Psychology and Religion: West and East*. 2nd ed. Translated by R. F. C. Hull. Bollingen Series XX. Princeton: Princeton University Press, 1963.
— Foreward and Commentary to *The Secret of the Golden Flower: A Chinese Book of Life*. Translated and explained by Richard Wilhelm. A Helen and Kurt Wolff Book. New York City: Harcourt, Brace & World, Inc., 1962.
— *The Spirit in Man, Art, and Literature*. Translated by R. F. C. Hull. Bollingen Series XX. New York City: Pantheon Books, 1966.
— *The Structure and Dynamics of the Psyche*. Translated by R. F. C. Hull. Bollingen Series XX. New York City: Pantheon Books, 1960.
— *Two Essays on Analytical Psychology*. Translated by H. G. and C. F. Baynes. London: Baillière, Tindall and Cox, 1928.

Works on Paul Claudel

Beaumont, Ernest. «Claudel and Sophia». *Claudel: A Reappraisal*. Edited by Richard Griffiths. Chester Springs, Pa.: Dufour Editions, 1968.
Blanchot, Maurice. *Le Livre à venir*. 4th ed. Paris: Gallimard, 1959.
Fumet, Stanislas. *Claudel*. 6th ed. La Bibliothèque idéale. Paris: Gallimard, 1958.
Howells, Bernard. «The enigma of *Partage de midi:* a study in ambiguity». *Claudel: A Reappraisal*. Edited by Richard Griffiths. Chester Springs, Pa.: Dufour Editions, 1968.
Kempf, Jean-Pierre and Petit, Jacques. «Études sur la 'trilogie' de Claudel: 1. *L'Otage*». Archives claudeliennes 5. *Archives des Lettres Modernes*, 69 (1966).
Labriolle, Jacqueline de. «Le thème de la rose». Paul Claudel 3: thèmes et images. *La Revue des Lettres Modernes*, 134-36 (1966), 65-106.
Meyer, Agnes. «Note-Book». *Claudel et l'Amérique II*. Edited by

Eugène Roberto. Cahier canadien Claudel 6. Ottawa: Éditions de l'Université d'Ottawa, 1969.

Petit, Jacques. *Claudel et l'usurpateur*. Paris: Desclée de Brouwer, 1971.

— «La structure». Paul Claudel 6: la premiere versión de *La Ville*. *La Revue des Lettres Modernes*, 209-11 (1969), 35-52.

Plourde, Michel. *Paul Claudel: Une Musique du silence*. Montréal: Les Presses de l'Université de Montréal, 1970.

Roberto, Eugène. «*Le Jet de pierre*». *Formes et figures*. Cahier canadien Claudiel 5. Ottawa: Éditions de l'Université d'Ottawa, 1967.

Vachon, André. *Le Temps et l'espace dans l'oeuvre de Paul Claudel: Expérience chrétienne et imagination poétique*. Paris: Éditions du Seuil, 1965.

Watanabé, Moriaki. «Le 'Don', ou la logique dramatique de *Partage de midi*». Paul Claudel 5: schémas dramatiques. *La Revue des Lettres Modernes*, 180-82 (1968), 25-58.

SE TERMINÓ DE IMPRIMIR EN
LA CIUDAD DE MADRID EN EL
MES DE SEPTIEMBRE DE 1977

studia humanitatis